Leander M. Zimmerman

Expository Thoughts on Pilgrim's Progress

Leander M. Zimmerman

Expository Thoughts on Pilgrim's Progress

ISBN/EAN: 9783337292850

Printed in Europe, USA, Canada, Australia, Japan

Cover: Foto ©Lupo / pixelio.de

More available books at **www.hansebooks.com**

Preface.

We are all Pilgrims in this world, for "this is not our home." . . . . Heaven is the goal toward which every thoughtful one aspires. Loved ones have gone before, and that the journey may be made all the more successful by those who yet remain, this little book is sent forth. . . . . May it prove a guiding light, a helping hand, a kind word to many weary travelers, that they may all the better "run with patience the race" that is set before them. . . . .

⁂ ⁂ ⁂ The Author.

CONTENTS.

Chapter.		Page.
I.	Flight From the City of Destruction,	5.
II.	The Wicket Gate,	15.
III.	Loosing the Burden at the Cross,	24.
IV.	Valley of Humiliation and Conflict with Apollyon,	34.
V.	Valley of Death and Break of Day,	42.
VI.	Vanity Fair,	52.
VII.	"Buy the Truth,"	60.
VIII.	Doubting Castle,	69.
IX.	Atheism—Scepticism—Infidelity,	78.
X.	Over the River into the Celestial City,	87.

FROM THE

CITY OF DESTRUCTION

TO THE

CELESTIAL CITY.

CHAPTER I.
FLIGHT FROM THE CITY OF DESTRUCTION.

THE book, and the only book, next to the Bible is Bunyan's Pilgrim's Progress. "That book brought me to the true light," is doubtless the experience of many of the followers of God to-day. Its author, like many great men, sprang from a very sinful youth; for Bunyan was a most depraved boy. He was so profane that even a bad woman of his native place, charged him with being so very wicked that he would corrupt all with whom he came in contact. His first reformation seems to have begun with his marriage to a godly woman. Like him, many men have been made great by such a marriage and it would be well for many others of the world to do likewise; that is, marry, but marry in the Lord. A godly wife, by her influence and example, can very often make of a worldly man, a man of God. Gradually, thereafter, Bunyan began to lop off one branch of sin after another, striving each day to become just a little better. It was not, however, until he overheard the conversation of two women, who were conversing about righteousness, that he discovered he was merely cutting off sinful branches without uprooting the tree of sin itself, in his soul. The conversation of those two women led him to serious reflection, and, seeing wherein he was weak, and learning of the true source of strength, he thereafter turned to the Fount of all blessings, Jesus, and became a true disciple of Christ.

How unfortunate it would have been, had those two women talked along the line of many gossipers, in dissecting the character of such as had been trying to serve God to the best of their ability, or had found fault with God, or spoken evil of the church and religion. Had they been such gossipers or faultfinders, Bunyan would doubtless never have written Pilgrim's Progress. It simply goes to show the importance of guarding well our speech, for conversation is often heard through the wall, as when Bunyan overheard the two women. You may be riding along in the street car speaking evil of a person, while just opposite sits some one drinking in every word you utter. You may be standing on the street corner gossiping about your next door neighbor, while in the adjoining house, seated at an open window, sits some one waiting to peddle out and spread the poisonous words you are uttering. You may be seated in the church talking about a member of the same congregation, while before or behind you may be sitting, unnoticed, a listener only too eager to herald abroad your conversation, causing mischief between friend and friend. When you least expect it, the conversation will be heard, either for good or evil.

Having thus been led to turn to a higher life through the godly conversation of the two women, Bunyan became a most ardent follower of Jesus Christ, and preached the Gospel of glad tidings. But, living in an age of martyrdom, he was soon persecuted for his good works, and, in all, spent twelve long years in prison. This was a sore disappointment to him, for he had planned to do so much for his Master, and now all his hopes seemed to vanish. Lodged in his place of confinement, he longed for some way of serving his Lord, and in the words of Job, he doubtless exclaimed, "Oh that my words were written, that they were printed in a book, that they were engraven with an iron pen in the rock forever." And then as if by inspiration, (for it would seem that the book is largely the work of inspiration) God sent an angel; in the hand of the author was placed a pen, and Bunyan wrote Pilgrim's Progress.

Thus his imprisonment proved to him a great blessing; for without the affliction, he would never have had this great inspiration given unto him. It is in like manner that the hours of imprisonment are often blessings in disguise. Without his confinement, Paul would never have given unto the world his richest Epistles. He might have preached parts of them to a few people, but they would never have been handed down to generation after generation. Being imprisoned, however, he wrote his thoughts and they were scattered abroad to feed thousands upon thousands. We often object to the thorn, but while we complain of it let us remember that at the very spot where there is a thorn, there is also a rose blooming; and as the thorn protects the rose not only from the storm but from the promiscuous touch of every passer-by, so the thorns of life may occasionally hurt us, yet at the same time they protect us and keep us from the violent storms of sin and temptation, preserving thus the very flower of piety, purity and character for the great garden of God at last in heaven. Otherwise many of the present blooming flowers in that heavenly garden, would long since have been plucked by evil hands, trampled under foot and cast into outer darkness. While in prison Bunyan received from God the rare blessing and privilege of giving to the world precious thoughts from precious leaves of the great book of life's experiences.

In his dream he beheld

"*A man in rags.*"

This at once suggests the picture of the unregenerate; for their state is represented as "filthy rags" in the sight of God. True, very many attempt to make a covering for their nakedness, but their efforts are as unsuccessful as were the efforts of Adam and Eve when they endeavored to cover themselves with fig leaves. One may hold a lofty position as a great ruler, and think thereby to be great, but unless he be a child of God, "washed in the blood of the Lamb," his greatness is as "filthy rags" in the sight of God. Another may try to clothe himself with the robe of self-righteousness, but unless that robe be made whiter than snow through the atoning mercies of Jesus Christ, that man is as unwelcome in the sight of God as the sinner that walks the streets; for unless the righteousness exceed that of the Scribes and Pharisees it is worthless. Another may try to weave for self a cloak of good works, but we are not saved by mere works of righteousness.

All such cloaks are but as "rags" in the eyes of God, and man stands condemned for his sins. Sin from its very nature clothes a man with "rags," both literally and spiritually. The prodigal could not travel many years in the way of sin before he was clothed in rags in the true sense of the term; and like him, many men and women are walking our streets in rags, because they have been traveling along the paths of transgression. It costs a good bit to be a sinner, and when the money is all spent, then all that sin gives to man is "rags" for his body and "husk" for his food. The very countenance of the sinner makes him known. Place ten good, pure, honest, upright young men or women together, and beside them place ten who are of the world, who find satisfaction in "eating, drinking and being merry," and you will readily be enabled to tell who are the good, and who are the bad. The very eye, the expression will bespeak the character of each. Compare the countenances of men and women in prisons and dens of iniquity, with those of men and women in churches, and you will have many living witnesses and proofs of the wages of sin as they appear in the wicked, while the righteous show by their very countenance that they are good and pure, for they have been cleansed and clothed in white robes of righteousness; the old man is put off with his "rags," and the new man put on with the robe of righteousness.

The man as seen by Bunyan was not only clothed in "rags," but he stood in a place with

"*His face from his own house.*"

That is the position of the man who is disgusted with the sins of this world and who is resolved to seek something better. It is the attitude of the man who starts out to follow Christ. He is leaving all to follow Jesus; and unless we forsake all we are not worthy of being called Christ's disciples. Not that the christian is expected to give up a legitimate business because he has become a christian, for it is just then that he is rather enjoined "to be diligent in business." God never intended His followers should be lazy men," or even "men and women of leisure."

Christianity does not lock up the doors of a man's place of business, nor does it say to man he must not be concerned about the same, but it does mean that man shall not make his business his God. It does mean that business shall be second, and that the Kingdom of God shall be sought first. It does mean that business shall be honestly carried on for the glory of God. Unhappily, too many are trying to follow God with one foot, while with the other they are endeavoring to follow the devil, but such method of travel is impossible. You cannot travel two roads that lead in opposite directions at the same time, nor can we "serve God and mammon" at the same time. To follow Christ means self-denial of time, money, pleasure, and of all, making thus the chief end of life the glorifying of God.

If many were to stop and ponder the path they are traveling, they would discover danger, for many are on dangerous soil. Were many of the professed followers of God, in His church at large, to drop dead suddenly in the district they are traveling, there would be a question as to where they belonged. The church would come forward and claim them, but on the other hand the devil would put forth his claims, demanding them on the ground that they had fallen upon his territory. Many of the world's pleasure-seekers, and many of the Marthas in the homes "cumbered solely about much serving" without regard to "the one thing needful," and many of the business people at large who are seeking everything else before they consider the demands of religion, would do well to reflect for a moment, whether or not they are "leaving all to follow Christ: whether or not they have "their face from their house," or whether they are not turned with their faces toward the world.

Too many are like Lot's wife, they are "fleeing from the wrath to come," yet worried about what they have left behind. With longings they look back, losing sight of the prize that is set before them, and in their thrist for the things of this life, they lose the blessing of heaven, and fall a prey into the hands of the enemy. Let go of sin, break loose from the clutches of the adversary, and with face turned toward Christ, and eyes fixed upon Him, run with patience the race that is set before you, ever looking unto Jesus as the Author of your faith. With such following after Christ, all the other needful things of life shall be added. The poorest kind of economy is that which takes away from God, for while God can live without man, man cannot live without God, and with God on our side, even the "littles" shall be blessed.

Cheap religion is as worthless as it is cheap, and no greater mistake can be made by any one than by trying to see how little it costs to get to heaven. Many seem to think they will do just as little as they possibly can for Christ, both in service and gifts, instead of doing all they possibly can. Only "the faithful servant" will reach heaven to receive the plaudit "well done." The fruitful tree is a great blessing to the hungry and weary traveler, but the barren fig tree, with its deceptive properties, a curse; accordingly such as profess to be followers of God, unless they are as the fruitful tree to feed others and bless them, then they will be rather of the barren fig tree order, to be a stumbling block, a curse, a hindrance to the cause of their Master. Some christians tell the truth when they sing, "Nothing in my hands I bring," for they are trying to get to heaven "empty handed" on "flowery beds of ease." Even were it possible for such ever to enter heaven, they would feel most uncomfortable there to look around and see others with their arms full of the golden grain gathered for the Master, and they themselves, "empty handed."

In his further description of the man as seen in his dream, Bunyan speaks of him as having

"A burden upon his back."

This is the condition of the man who is under conviction. The wreckless sinner who heedlessly goes on sinning without any thought, for a time feels perhaps little of this burden, but when once man stops and considers the folly of his way, then he is made to feel the weight of sin. His conscience condemns him, and he feels his guilt in the sight of God. Such as consider, are made aware of their guilt, and are conscious of the burden that rests upon their souls. If only more would stop for a time and seriously ponder, they would see their mistakes, and would turn from evil doing. Such are likely to count the cost of sin, and seeing that "the wages of sin is death," will feel the awful weight of the same. But even those who do not seriously consider, sooner or later are made to feel the burden of sin, for at first the weight may be comparatively light, but gradually it grows heavier until at last it becomes a burden. How many, like Samson, have walked off with the gates of sin at first! But, in the end, the strongest have been overpowered by the burden, and like that giant in strength, were crushed by the ruins of a life not well spent. Sin may be light for a time and some have thereby boasted of its pleasures, but the eyes of many are opened when too late. Shorn of their strength, they are left to tread in the mill of despair and shame, a laughing stock to the world, and a misery to self. The sins of an evening weigh most heavily upon the soul at night, as the transgressor lies down in his room alone to sleep. His pillow seems full of thorns, while his heart is weary and heavy laden with the burden of sin. It is verily true that "the way of the transgressor is hard."

Happily for the man, seen by Bunyan in his dreams, he had
"*A book in his hand*"
which was God's word. This book told him of the light and the life that Christ came into this world to give unto man. If people would read more generally the Bible, there would not be so many in darkness and sin. The Bible is a Light to lead souls out of darkness, and point them to Jesus as the Lamb of God, that taketh away the sins of the world, but how shall men know of the Way and the Truth and the Life, unless they hear and read God's Word? "Faith cometh by hearing," and the Bible "is the lamp unto our feet, and light unto our pathway."

It was under circumstances of this kind that Bunyan describes man awakened by the Divine Light of God's Word; and seeing the dangerous ground upon which he was standing, the awakened sinner informed his wife of his unrest and desire for the true Light. But alas, like many other foolish and unbelieving wives, she only ridiculed the idea of her husband, and plead with him to remain where he was, in the City of Destruction; for to her there was no danger, as she thought. The wife can do much toward the making of her husband, a follower of either the Lord or the devil. If the wife is not religiously inclined, and if she be concerned only about the home, she cannot expect her husband to be a very faithful christian. Hence many wives by their example are virtually drawing their husbands back into the world. But woe is that one who thus sins away her day of grace, while at the same time she, perhaps, keeps another soul away from the fold of Christ?

But the man referred to by Bunyan was wise in that when it came to a matter of his own soul's welfare, he would rather forsake his wife than live in sin, and appear a condemned criminal at the bar of God. Although one member of the family may be an unbeliever, yet that is no reason why another should deny God and sell his soul to the devil. When it is a matter of the salvation of the soul, each one is personally responsible for his or her own redemption.

Better, by far, to do as did Bunyan's Christian, when putting his fingers to his ears that he might not hear the Syren voice he ran crying,

"*Life, life, eternal life,*"

for he had received the commission to "flee from the wrath to come," which warning is given to every unregenerate man and woman.

No one has an excuse for not having been warned, for the Gospel call has gone forth in this christian land of ours, so that every one who has had any desire to be saved, could be if he would. It is not true that many are in sin because "no man careth for their souls," for the preached word, and the written word, all tell of God's love, and admonish the sinner "to flee from the wrath" of God.

Every effort is being put forth to reach the masses, and "whosoever will, may come." Even "the Spirit and the Bride say, Come." And it is enjoined upon all who have heard, to say, "Come." But for fear some one might not hear the call, it is written, "Let him that is athirst come." But, lest even then there be one who might claim that he personally had not been invited to come to the Master, it is written, " Whosoever will, may come." That means every sinner. If you as a reader are not yet saved, then, it means *you* personally. But while the call is so general, yet, it is imperative, for there is great danger in delay. To-morrow may be too late to begin to start on the journey for heaven. "This very night thy soul may be required of thee." "The wrath of God" is often nearer than is expected, and many have thought it afar off, when the breath of fever laid them low upon the sick couch, and before they had time to make their peace with Him, they have been ushered unprepared into His very presence, to receive the doleful sentence, "Depart from me, for I never knew you." What an awful condition for the soul of the dying not to be saved! How bitter the lamentation of such, "The harvest is past, the summer ended, and I am not saved." How sad that bitter wail, "Almost, but lost!"

CHAPTER II.
THE WICKET GATE.

HAPPILY for Christian, he was met by a kind friend who directed him in the right way, so that he once more could renew his journey with courage and delight. From his sad experience of allowing himself to be lured from the right path by a man of the world, he became suspicious of any that might meet him along the road, and he turned back to the right way in great haste, for he realized that he was on forbidden ground; he also refused to look either to the right or to the left, lest he might step aside from the proper course.

It would indeed be well if more would profit, not only by the sad experience of Bunyan's Christian, but even by their own, for all who have stepped aside from the path of righteousness have discovered that they are on forbidden and dangerous ground, as well as that they have done that which is harmful to them, and the quicker they get back into the way of the Lord, the better. Not only let such wayward ones return, but return in haste and fear, looking neither to the right nor to the left for things of the world, but hasten back into the way the Lord would have them go.

Having safely reached the path, Christian soon came to
"*The gate*"
to which he had been directed. That gate was to represent Christ as the only way, the door. Says Christ, "I am the door; by me if any man enter in, he shall be saved, and shall go in and out, and find pasture." Again He says, "I am the way; and no man cometh unto the Father, but by me." Unhappily there are many who try other ways of getting to heaven. One

says, "I observe the Golden Rule as the guide of my faith, and that is good enough for any one." Another says, "I have never wronged any one, and of what have I to repent? I have ever lived a good, moral life, and that is all that is needful." Another tries the way of the Formalist, and thinks that by reading his Bible and Prayer Book, he will get to heaven. These are, however, not the gates to glory that God speaks of. They may all be good as helps to glory, but Christ, and Christ only, is the hope of glory. He is the Way, the Gate, and no one can enter heaven by any other way.

One of the conditions for admission at this "Gate" is to "knock," as did Christian. Although God knows what we need before we make a request of Him, yet, we are commanded to "ask" if we would "receive." Some people are anxious for certain things, but they are too proud to ask for them. They may throw all manner of hints, but are not willing to openly ask. This is the way with many who come to Christ for the pardon of their sins. They are desirous of receiving the forgiveness of their iniquity, but they make known their request in such an obscure manner that the Lord Himself fails to recognize their wishes. All manner of things are spoken of, and asked for, save the one thing needful. If the Lord would open the "door" without their "knocking," it might be acceptable with such persons, but they do not want to put themselves in the position of having to "knock" and "ask." But "knocking and asking" are not the only essentials. Another requisite for passing through the Door of Mercy is, confession. Christian said to the one who met him at the gate, "Here is a poor burdened sinner." That is the attitude that should characterize every one that seeks the forgiveness of his sins; for, "if we confess our sins God is faithful and just to forgive us our sins, and to cleanse us from all unrighteousness." But here again too many are unwilling to acknowledge their sins. They will not admit having done wrong, and of course with such a spirit they cannot be penitent, and without repentance there can be no forgiveness of sins; for, how can God forgive sins, if man refuses to admit that he is a sinner who needs forgiveness?

Pride thus keeps many away from Christ, because they are not willing to confess their errors. It is not a pleasant thing for one to confess his wrong, and yet, it is the only way we can ever expect forgiveness.

A rather singular experience occurred to Christian as he was about to enter the "Gate." He was taken by the hand and quickly pulled in through the open way, and when he asked to know the reason, he was told of a Castle near by, where dwelt one who was jealous of all who entered by way of the "Gate," and to prevent such from entering, would shoot forth arrows after them, if perchance he might prevent the entrance. This is more or less the experience of every one who is about to pass through the Door of Mercy; for Satan is the great enemy, ever "seeking whom he may devour," and all manner of darts are hurled to prevent the young and old from becoming followers of the Lord and Saviour, Jesus Christ. As long as men and women live *in* and *of* the world, the devil does not annoy them but gradually, blindly leads them on into the way that leadeth unto death. But let any become conscious of their danger and "flee from the wrath to come." Let them knock at the Door of Mercy, and confess their sins, then Satan at once applies his arts and skill in endeavoring to lure such back, by promising them all manner of pleasure, and pointing out to them the hardships of a christian life. It is dangerous, therefore, for any to be indifferent or lurking in their approach unto the Lord, for unless there be a firm resolve to follow after the Lord, Satan will tempt such to delay until a "more convenient season," which, in all probability, will be never. To become a true follower of Christ one must be sincere, in earnest, seeking "Life, life, eternal life" as the chief aim.

Many indeed, start out for heaven in company with others, but at last enter heaven all alone. Because their friends grew lukewarm and indifferent, and turned back again into the world, as did Pliable who followed Christian for a short journey, so, meeting with discouragements, many turn back. Alas, how often is this true in life? Many husbands and wives starting for the heavenly home together, parted before reaching the end of the journey, one patiently running the race set before them, while the other grew weary in well doing, and returned to the world, the flesh, and the devil. Or, perhaps it was a brother and sister who started together at the altar, at the time of their confirmation or profession of faith. For a short time they traveled together, but one or the other became careless and indifferent, turning back to the place from whence they came, while the other was left to go alone along the way to glory. Many thus start together in churches, kneeling beside each other at the same altar, professing Christ at the same time, but one by one of the number drifts away, and falls back into the world again, leaving the "few that be saved" to continue on in the good way they started. A call of the roll in every church would disclose such facts, and what sad facts they are! Thus, congregations, families, and friends, start together on the heavenly journey, yet how many are left to enter heaven alone because others have renounced the faith by neglect and willful sins!

Having passed in through the "Gate," Christian was pointed to
" *The straight and narrow way* "
and ordered to pursue it. After all, there is but one *right* way, and that road is "straight and narrow." The way of the world is so broad that "many go that way." It is so easy, that without effort many travel it. It requires prudence and effort to keep in the "narrow path that leads unto life everlasting," and for that reason it is written, "Strive to enter," implying the effort required. A thousand and one different paths cross and recross the "narrow way" and unless the pilgrim is watchful of his steps and attentive to the instructions given at the start, he will step aside from the right path into the way of sin and death. All along the way are Syren voices and temptations to lure the christian aside from that which is holy.

Keeping in the "narrow way" Christian finally came to a beautiful dwelling known as
" *The house of the Intrepreter.* "
This was to represent the work of the Holy Spirit, in revealing to man the things that make wise unto salvation, by awakening within him, not only the conviction of sin, but the danger of falling away from grace.

In the house of the Interpreter Christian was shown a room into which was called a man who swept it. This created so very much dust, that Christian was almost choked. Then water was sprinkled

 in the room and the dust settled. This clearly represented the futile effort of the law to cleanse the soul of sin, and the need of the Gospel of Love to wash and cleanse; it also illustrates the condition of many whose christian experience is most sorely neglected. The soul might be represented as having different apartments, but unhappily, "the parlor" as in the house of the Interpreter, is frequently neglected. The very best part is allowed to become covered with the dust of neglect. Some professors of religion think it sufficient if they serve Christ only in part, retaining for their own use whatever they may deem advisable. Such persons but naturally reserve for themselves the best, "the parlor," while they dedicate to Christ the "kitchen," the crumbs and off-falls.

It is no wonder that when the Lord comes to such and gives them a good sweeping by the Gospel of true consecration that the very dust is such as to almost "choke" the poor unfortunate creatures, for in their slothfulness the dust has so accumulated that when once the Lord takes hold of them, they are surprised to see how dusty and corrupt have become their lives. No wonder that at death many such quake, fear and tremble, since their condition is a miserable illustration of their past neglect.

In that same house of the Interpreter, Christian was further shown another room in which sat two children, each one on a chair. Their names were respectively,

"*Passion and Patience.*"

The one, Passion, was eager for every thing he could lay his hands on, while Patience sat willing to wait for the time when he was to receive what belonged to him. It so happened, therefore, that at the time when Patience began to receive his portion of good things, then Passion had consumed all his and had utterly nothing left. What a revelation of such as are concerned in this life only for the things which satisfy for the present! Many like Dives have their day of good things now, to the envy of others. They have every thing the heart could possibly crave, and regardless of the hereafter, they "eat, drink and are merry," while others, who are looked upon as less fortunate, have little more than "the crumbs that fall from the rich man's table." The man of the world has his good things now, while the Christian is patiently waiting for his best to begin at the time when the man of the world has nothing left. The pleasures of sin at best are but for a very short season, and then, like the child "Passion," they in turn have anguish and remorse, while the "good things" that await the Christian are everlasting.

The christian, therefore, needs to learn to be patient, and not grow weary in well doing: "for in due season we shall reap, if we faint not." While godliness is profitable unto all things, having even the promise of the life that now is, (for such as faithfully serve God are truly profited in this present life,) yet, the best is kept in store for the christian until the next life. The path of the just, accordingly, does not only "shine more and more" as each day passes by, but "unto the perfect day," the day when the christian shall realize the force of the words of the Psalmist, when he wrote, saying: "I shall be satisfied when I awake in thy likeness."

There was still another room in the house of the Interpreter that greatly impressed Christian, for in it he saw a fire burning beside a wall, and although a man stood there pouring water on the flame, yet, it burned higher and hotter. Upon investigation, however, it was discovered that unseen, just behind the wall, stood another who was quietly and constantly pouring oil into the fire.

This is a forcible illustration of the manner in which the grace of God works in the heart of man. While the grace is there as the gift of God, yet Satan stands pouring upon it all manner of hindrances, such as might put out the flames of love, kindled in the heart. Once a christian, does not mean that the work is forever done, for there is need of constant attention lest the fires upon the altar of the heart die out, and nothing but the dark ashes of a sinful life remain, instead. Too many seem to think that when once they have knelt at the altar, and there made a public profession of their faith in the Lord, that then all is done, and they have nothing more to do. As well say, when a young man leaves College with his Diploma, that then all his work is done, as to say that the mere profession of Christ concludes the christian's work. The diploma does not make a man a Physician, Lawyer or Minister. When a man graduates from college he first begins his life's work. And so it is with young converts; they are only beginning their work in the Master's Vineyard, and unless they are conscious of this fact, and at once go to work for Jesus, they will soon allow their faith to die out, for Satan stands ready to extinguish the spark of life as kindled upon the altar of the heart by Christ. It is because of this, that Christ, Himself, like the unseen man, stands by the christian constantly fanning into flames, the oil of salvation which He adds to the young convert in and through the means of grace. It is, accordingly, often asked why certain ones are enabled to stand so firm for Christ. The answer might well be given by saying, it is because they themselves are true to their trust, faithful upon the means of grace, and hence, although unseen by the outside world, yet, Christ stands constantly by the side of the faithful "so that as their day, so is their strength." Such as are faithful to their trust may take assurance from on high in Christ's own promise when He said, "I will not leave nor forsake you. Lo I am with you always."

A last scene in the house of the Interpreter that specially moved Christian was that of a man who was shut up in an iron cage in a dark room. The best explanation of this is given in the man's own words, as to why he was there thus in misery. "I left off to watch and be sober; I laid the reins upon the neck of my lusts; I sinned against the light of the word, and the goodness of God; I have grieved the Spirit and He is gone; I tempted the devil and he is come to me; I have so hardened my heart that I cannot repent."

What an awful but real picture of the backslider! Shakespeare expresses this condition when he says:

"In the corrupted currents of this world, offence's gilded hand may shove by justice; and oft 'tis seen, the wicked purse itself buys out the law; but," says he, "'tis not so above: There is no shuffling, there the action lies in his true nature; and we ourselves compelled, even to the teeth and forehead of our faults, to give in evidence."

And what an evidence for many at the final day! The same poet asks:

> "What then? what rests?
> Try what repentence can; what it cannot?
> Yet, what can it, when one cannot repent?
> O wretched state! O bosom, black as death!
> O lined soul, that struggling to be free,
> Art more engaged! Help, angels! make assay:
> Bow, stubborn knees, and, heart, with strings of steel,
> Be soft as sinews of the new-born babe."

Yes, bow humbly before God if you are a backslider, and there implore His forgiveness, lest your experience be that of others who have gone before you. After all, there is nothing in the world with its sinful allurements, for the dejected man in the iron cage expressed his disappointment in the words, "The lust, pleasures, and profits of this world; in the enjoyment of which I did then promise myself much delight: but now every one of those things also bite me, and gnaw me like a burning worm."

Few persons ever get much satisfaction out of sin, but very many find in it only "sorrow and vexation of spirit." No one, therefore, needs to experiment with sin for the sake of experience, for the history of many unfortunates suffices to prove sin a great curse.

Every one should accordingly take heed to his conduct and walk in life, and not leave off the duties of a christian for the pleasures of the world and selfish gratification, lest unawares the reins be laid upon the neck of sinful lust, and the Holy Spirit grieved. The multiplication of little neglects of duty, and the committing of little sins, finally form a habit for evil doing, and gradually, and unconsciously the grieved Spirit takes His flight, and the backslider is eft alone, his heart so hardened as to render it impossible for the unfortunate ever more to repent. Thus, such are left like the abandoned vessel, from which has gone forth the captain; the anchor is cut loose from its moorings, while the vessel is left to drift, and drift on out into the great sea, at last to sink into the great deep, and be lost.

Thus, the soul that grieves the Holy Spirit, causing the Spirit to take His flight, is cut loose from its moorings upon the Rock Christ

Jesus, and Christ as the Captain of salvation has gone forth from the soul, while in its wrecked condition it drifts on out into the dark, drifting on and on, until at last the soul dashes out of sight into outer darkness. Suppose that soul be the soul of your father or mother, or the soul of your brother or sister! Suppose that it were your *own* soul! "Grieve not the Holy Spirit of God, whereby ye are sealed unto the day of redemption," but rather earnestly appeal to the Holy Spirit for help, crying out in deep sincerity:

'Come, Holy Spirit, Heavenly Dove,
With all thy power divine,
Kindle a flame of sacred love,
In this cold heart of mine.'

CHAPTER III.
LOOSING THE BURDEN AT THE CROSS.

CHRISTIAN finally departed from the "House of Interpretation," and resumed his journey along a road, on either side of which was a wall. This would remind us of the way of salvation which is in a large sense a "walled highway," up which the traveler to Zion is to journey. While there are many opportunities to step aside from the right path, nevertheless, in a large measure God protects it for the christian with the walls of salvation so as to hedge up the way, and thereby keep the christian from being lured away into paths of sin. Often Providence hedges up a man's way with "thorns," not from hatred, but from love. The hedge along the roadside is to keep the traveler in the right path, and such as press through it into some other way are usually punished for the same from the bruises incurred by such violation. This is the manner of God in protecting our way to glory, and such as press through the "hedge" suffer, for the "way of the transgressor is hard." In order to save many from such wanderings, God places along the wayside "hedges" in the form of sickness, misfortune, bereavement, all of which wall up the way of the traveler so as to keep him in the path that leads to the land where sorrow is unknown.

Following along the "walled highway" Christian went on with the "burden" upon his back until at last he came to a Cross. Standing before it, in deep penitence, he beheld a chasm near its base and there

Before the Cross he lost his Burden.

This is to teach us of the power of the Cross of Christ. Many are they who are bearing burdens. There is a mighty army of sinners bearing loads so heavy that they are being crushed beneath the weight of their transgressions. Sin is a most grievous burden, and beneath its weight many fall crushed to death, to appear before the bar of God without pardon. Such, however, as feel their burden of sin, sorely repenting of the same, going to Christ for the removal of that burden, such find relief, for Christ is the One to remove all burdens. If, therefore, those who are in sin would go to Christ, and there before Him unbosom all, and having thus made a clear confession, be truly sorry and ask God's forgiveness, they could, like Christian of old, walk away with the burden rolled from their heart and soul. God does not stop to inquire into the greatness of the sin, but into the nature of the confession and repentance of the sinner, and such as come in the proper spirit of meekness and humility, receive the entire forgiveness of their sins, even though their sins may have been as scarlet, or red as crimson. When once God has forgiven and Christ washed those sins in His own blood through His Atonement, then those very sins of scarlet and crimson, become as snow and as wool, for they have been washed and made white in the blood of the Lamb. The great misfortune with many is they want to wash away their sins with their own bloody hands, and when they have finished their effort, they discover the leprous spots still remain. Nothing but the blood of Jesus can atone for our sins, and God Himself realized this fact, otherwise why would He have required the death of His only beloved Son to atone for the sins of the world? For centuries the world tried other methods, but none could make the comers thereunto perfect. Only Christ could make full atonement.

But there are other burdens than sin, under which many are oppressed. Doubt, hangs upon the hearts of many like a heavy weight. When Thomas doubted the testimony of the disciples concerning the fact of Christ's resurrection, he had upon his heart a burden of which the world never knew, for he was the one of the eleven to refuse to believe in the resurrection. When, however, he saw the risen Saviour, then there was rolled from him a burden, the burden of unbelief. To bear long that burden is to become dwarfed in christian experience, and the weight of it will drag down the soul to darkness and infidelity. There is also the burden of sorrow that hangs heavily upon the souls of many. What an army of sorrowing mortals are marching along the highway of life. The very countenance of many tells of the burden of sorrow at heart, while there are still others who, apparently happy, yet, have sorrows known only to themselves and their God. Smiles as they appear upon the faces of many are forced, while deep down in the soul, hidden from the world, there lies the secret germ of sorrow, doing deadly work. There is also the burden of bereavement that has weighed down many into conditions that hasten on the heavy-laden to untimely graves. Rachels weeping for their children, because they are not, and Naomis traveling along the great highway of life, apparently "empty" of all that would cheer life's journey. Then, too, there is a class of persons bearing the burden of despondency, which has proven a millstone to drag many down to an untimely death. Many such are hiding away in the wilderness of loneliness and misery, desiring rather to die and depart than to live and face life's conflict. The charms of life to them appear to have vanished, while the rugged path and the thorny way seem all that is left.

Once they had many friends, but now they are all gone. Once they had plenty of this world's goods, but their wealth has vanished like the dew before the rising sun. Once they were kindly greeted and even courted, but now they, like Diogenes of old, are compelled to look with a lantern at broad daylight for some one who would be willing to lend a helping hand. Once hope was bright, but now it is a stranger. Stranded thus amid these unfortunate surroundings, man is often heavily burdened, and some such would even blow out the candle of life, rather than see it flicker in the few remaining drops of oil. But before all these, there is a place where they may come and find relief. It is at the Cross of Christ.

"At the cross, and beneath it only,
Finds the troubled heart relief,
There's a balm beneath its shadow,
That can soothe all earthly griefs.

"Trials come and tempests scatter,
All our earthly hopes to dust,
Yet we find relief and refuge,
'Neath the cross of Him we trust.

"Oh, how sweet to know that ever,
We've a friend that loves us true,
Who will never, never leave us,
Never veil His cross from view.

> "Blessed Saviour, wilt Thou ever,
> Keep us humbly at Thy cross,
> Hiding ever 'neath its shadow,
> Counting all beside but dross.
>
> "Blessed cross on which our Saviour,
> Bled and died that we might live,
> Unto all who hide beneath it,
> He eternal life will give."

If only more of the burdened of life would go to Christ, and there unbosom all to that Friend that loves even better than a brother, then there would be far less wounded at heart, and more happy saints of the Lord here on earth.

Scarcely had Christian thus knelt at the cross, before

"*Three Shining Ones*"

appeared to him, bidding him peace. He was then divested of his raiment and a new outfit given him instead. He was not first scolded for his sins, but was lovingly forgiven upon his proper repentance, and while he was deprived of that which he wore yet he was supplied with something far better.

So Christ deals with His followers. When He asks a man to deny self and become a follower of Him, Christ does not ask for all man may happen to cherish and give him nothing in return, but for the few crumbs man gives Christ, he in return receives the loaves, and for the few rags he gives, he in return receives that which, beside making him feel most comfortable, makes him appear most honorable in the sight of all men. The young man who left the swine herd for a sumptuous repast at his father's table, did not make a very great sacrifice. It is no sacrifice, for the same reason, for one to give up the pleasures of the world for the gift of eternal life, for when once that gift has been bestowed, then all "other things" are added. The men or the women of the world do not know what God has in store for those that love Him, for never having tasted of the good things of Christ, they are looking through a glass darkly. If many of our young men and women would

more sincerely consecrate themselves to Christ and His service, they would discover pleasures unspeakable, for while the world may give momentary gratification, the Gospel of Christ gives pleasure and satisfaction at a time when the world can do nothing for us. Moses, therefore, very wisely refused the pleasures of sin which were "but for a season," choosing instead "the afflictions of God's people" that in the end he might have eternal joy and happiness.

In order that Christian might not wander from the path, but have pointed out to him the proper way,

He was given a "Roll"

which told of the journey and the proper way, while at the same time a "Seal" was placed upon his forehead. God would not have His followers left in darkness as to what is their duty, but His Word is given "as a lamp unto their feet and a light unto their pathway."

"Whenever I am in doubt, or when I am discouraged, I read my Bible, and somehow I find in it that which helps me," is doubtless the experience of many. God's word is a most essential Guide Book on our way to the Heavenly City, and the more familiar we are with it, and the more we observe its instructions, the more progress will we make in our journey, and the less regrets will we have at the end of the way. The proper use of the Bible will help to preserve the seal of God's pardoning love upon the heart, as placed there by the power of the Holy Ghost, whereby we "are sealed unto the day of redemption." Neglect the "roll" of God's word, and the seal of the covenant of grace will sooner or later be broken. Dusty Bibles in the home are often indicative of broken "seals" of grace. It does not speak well for a christian to be indifferent to his or her Bible. Nor should the Bible be stored away like medicine to be used only when occasion demands. Many are the spiritual ills which might be avoided if more time were spent in reading the Divine Truth, and less time spent in reading much of the poisonous literature of the day. Many negligent christians in this respect fall asleep, like the three men whom Christian met. He tried with great difficulty to arouse them, but, half asleep each one offered an excuse and asked to be left alone "for a little more sleep."

Alas, how like many in life, who, instead of dilligently "running the race before them," are fast asleep! Many such are indeed "like them that sleep on the top of a mast." They are exposed to the greatest danger, not knowing at what moment an unexpected storm may arise and they be hurled to despair, yet, they appear unconscious of all danger and imminent peril. Death overtakes many as a thief in the night, and when least prepared, they are called to appear at the bar of God for the final rendering of their accounts. Only the last will avails, making all former null and void. This is also true in a spiritual sense. The mere fact of having made a "will" at the time of conversion and confession of Christ, does not guarantee a passport into heaven. It depends upon the life of the person after the will has been made. Each day, in a sense, man makes a different will to God. His actions, words, and whole life's conduct constitute the will, and although man may not literally write it, yet, the angel of the Lord records all, and the last day of a man's life forms in a large sense his final will, and unless, therefore, he prove "faithful unto death" he cannot expect the "crown of life."

But Christian himself unfortunately fell into a deep sleep. As in all important undertakings there are

"*Hills of Difficulty*"

to ascend, so in the way to the Celestial City, there are some parts of the road that require special effort to reach the summit. While there is much to stimulate, there is also much to discourage, and unless the follower of the Lord be in earnest, he will grow weary before he reaches the end of his journey. When, therefore, Christian was ascending a steep hill, and found midway up a beautiful arbor, he sat down in the cool shade and rested. It was a temptation to which many others would have yielded. In fact, Satan seems often to prepare just such places along the way of the christian pilgrim, if perchance he might thereby cause man to stop for a time from his christian activities. Many have thus gone on for a time faithfully serving God and His cause, until at last a seeming opportunity presented itself for them to discontinue their work, and, like Christian of old, they sat down to rest for a time. It is so very natural that it is frequently practiced. But, alas, Christian lived to regret his decision! So long as he rested from his journey and slept in the arbor he was doubtless satisfied, but when once his eyes were opened to the real condition of affairs, then he most bitterly lamented his having stopped by the way, for in his slumber he accidentally lost the Roll from his bosom where it had been kept, and when later on in his journey he was beset with dangers and reached for the Roll he found it was missing. But he searched in vain, for it could no where be found. He at once began to retrace his steps, and did not find the Roll until he came back to the arbor where he had slept. Then was there sore regret, for he realized the lost time and the many unnecessary steps which were required, because of his having slept at the shady nook. No wonder that he lamented, saying, "O that I should sleep in the day time!" And so, many will sooner or later utter the same lament, for in their day of grace they have no time to idly sleep away their precious hours, but are rather enjoined to "redeem the time," and not "be at ease in Zion."

Such as hang their harps on the willows, and sit down to rest while there is yet work to be done, will have no lawful excuse to offer God at the hour of judgment; and at a time when they least expect the importance of faithful consecration, they will discover the folly of having sinned away opportunities of grace.

There may arise discouragements by the way, yet discouragements are no excuse for slothfulness in the Master's service, for Christ Himself was "a man of sorrows," but He never ceased to do His Father's will. Notwithstanding there were some, and even many to oppose Him in His work, nevertheless, He ever "went about doing good," and would not cease to "do the will of the Father" merely because some people didn't like Him. Even though all forsook Him and fled, yet He was true to His mission and did not abandon the work He began, but was "faithful unto death." And, says the apostle, "Let the mind which was in Christ be also in you," and seek not your own pleasure.

When once the day of wrath shall come, and man be found wanting in the sight of God, then he will have only regrets for not having been faithful to the trust assigned him. And even such as sleep by the way, and afterward are enabled to receive the pardon of

God for their folly, should life be prolonged enough, yet, what is the lament! Surely, there can be no satisfaction for a christian man or woman who has opportunity to serve God, to sit idly by and watch others, and then at the close of life, repent of the sins, and go along the journey with the regret, "O that I had not slept!" "How many steps have I taken in vain!" Many have thus wandered from the way to glory to regret later the folly of thus having to start the journey over again, while others are cut down without an opportunity of retracing their steps, and beginning anew the way to the new life as it is in Christ Jesus our Lord.

Happily for Christian, he found the Roll again. He was then more eager than ever to resume his journey, for he was fearful of the results of such experiences.

Presently there loomed up before him in the distance the appearance of a most beautiful Palace. This was indeed an unexpected pleasure to him, for, doubtless, he felt he was not deserving of such happy glimpses so soon after his unfortunate experience, and yet, it taught him that just beyond where we are often tempted to turn back, there lies

The "palace beautiful,"

where God has in store for us rich blessings. Many, indeed, have turned back almost in sight of home, and been denied that which a few more efforts would have achieved.

The abandoned mine has often great riches just a few feet below the depth already dug, and so many have ceased their service for the Master just at a time when bright glimpses were about to appear and happy returns for all sacrifice made. But before reaching these beautiful places along life's journey we must not forget there are "lions" to pass, which are alongside the way. Nor is it wise to turn back because such "lions" may appear dangerous, for if we are truly sincere in our work, then the "lions" can do us no harm, but will be, as they were for Christian, "chained." Troubles often ise up before us like lions along the way of life, until at times it appears as if we could go no farther, but we should trust in God and faithfully go ahead, for "the lions are chained." Many have thus gone on past the lions along life's pathway, greatly trembling, when at the same time there was the "still small voice" calling to them, "fear no danger."

Press on then nobly amid all the trials of life, for although they may appear as "lions," yet they are chained, and Christ says, "Fear not for when thou passest through the waters, I will be with thee, and when thou walkest through the fire thou shalt not be burned. Lo, I am with you always."

> E'en through death's valley I should trod
> And there give up a friend to God,
> Yet why should I tremble and fear
> For Christ my Friend is very near.
>
> In days of grief He by me stood,
> And always has been very good.
> When night was dark and all things drear,
> Yet Christ my Friend stood very near.
>
> Oh anxious soul lift up gloom's veil,
> For Christ's strong arm will never fail.
> Then why tremble and be in fear,
> For Christ your Friend is very near.

CHAPTER IV.
VALLEY OF HUMILIATION AND CONFLICT WITH APOLLYON.

CHRISTIAN finally arrived at the House Beautiful and received a most delightful reception. Indeed he might well feel repaid for all he encountered, for it was such a lovely place that he appeared almost unwilling to leave it. In a certain sense this is true of the faithful worshipper of God in the Church, the Palace Beautiful. It is such a beautiful place that we are there enjoined to "worship the Lord in the beauty of holiness," and the Psalmist when opportunity afforded, was glad when they said unto him "let us go into the house of the Lord." Many indeed have since then realized the truth of his own sweet experience, for to sincere and faithful christians, worship in God's Sanctuary affords them their chief pleasure. Many are the happy experiences in God's house, and songs of praise to Him are there sung as only the pure in heart know the joy thereof. As in the "House Beautiful" Christian was met by most holy persons, who had charge of the place, so in God's house where the name of the Lord is recorded, there the Lord Himself meets with his people according to His promise to meet with even "two or three gathered in His name," and where the Lord records His name, there he is waiting to greet His people. It is this that makes a place of worship different from all other gatherings, for God is there to meet with such as have assembled in His name. His presence is a benediction, so that the Lord being in his holy temple, the earth but naturally keeps silent so far as worldly matters are concerned in the Church of God. The world is left on the outside, or at least should be, while the church is a place for service and worship of God. Things pertaining to the world and business concerns, should not be carried into the church by the worshippers.

It is an offence to God for any one to come before Him in worship in the sanctuary with the mind and heart full of worldly plans.

Nor should there be uttered in God's house at worship, those things which would tend to take the mind from things holy. Unhappily, Satan often has given unto him a large field for his mission, for while the word of God is preached, yet, many receive it as on stony places, and before they have reached their homes from the place of worship, they have allowed the devil to gather up all the good seed that was sown.

In the House Beautiful, Christian was asked why he had not brought along with him his wife and children. His answer was that which is common to many of even the present day. As regards his wife, she would not go with him, because she was unwilling to give up the things of the world. Like Lot's wife of old, she seemed to think more of worldly matters than of things spiritual. Nor was she alone in this respect, for like her, many other wives seem more concerned about "much serving" than about the "one thing needful." The wife is not required of God to neglect her household duties, but rather enjoined to "look well to the ways of her own household." And yet, to make the care of her household affairs her god, or her very first and chief consideration, is a great mistake, for she has enjoined upon her to "seek first the kingdom of God and his righteousness," and then all these other things "shall be added unto" her. Then too, Christian's children had a very common excuse for refusing to follow after their father in the service of the Lord. They were "given to the foolish, delights of youth." Youth has its foolish delights and very many of the young give way to these empty pleasures.

To speak to many young people about the "foolish delights of youth" is almost a waste of breath, for they refuse to be convinced that the delights are "foolish." They will listen, many of them, to the exhortations and warnings, but it is like pouring water into a sieve, for it is soon all gone, they fail to retain any of the good counsel. They resolve first to try for themselves, but many soon learn to know great disappointment and regret. In some matters experience is a very expensive teacher, and a long time is often required to pay the bill, to say nothing of the shame and remorse.

Before Christian resumed his journey he was sent into an armory where he was "harnessed from head to foot." Doubtless at the time he failed to appreciate the need of being thus protected, but later on he discovered that without such a previous preparation, he would have fallen a prey to the enemy. All manner of devices have been used for making life-saving garments. Even to-day many are secretly wearing such means of defense against the assasin's bullet or dagger. But what are all such dangers compared with the spiritual wounds that are being daily received by the multitude. Not only are the rich and rulers exposed to such "fiery darts" from the enemy, but the poorest and the humblest all are thus exposed. Beelzebub was ready from his castle to hurl the arrows, and since the day that the devil watched his opportunity to capture Eve, he has ever since been secretly watching for the best opportunity to capture the unwary and innocent. David felt the poisoned arrow as it pierced deep into his very soul, and filled him with bitter remorse. Peter was captured by the assassin, the devil, even to denying his own Master, and was saved at last only by the mercy of the Lord, saved as "a brand plucked from the fire." The christian armor, therefore, is an essential matter for the security of the man who would safely reach the Celestial City.

Thus equipped, Christian started to descend a steep hill. In doing so he was warned against the danger of the descent. And he discovered the need of the warning before he had entirely descended into

The Valley of Humiliation,

for while it is hard to ascend the Hill "Difficulty," it is equally dangerous to descend into the Valley of Humiliation, and like Christian, many stumble in the effort. It is no easy matter for one to step down from a high place of prominence into an obscure place of humiliation. Few people like to be told to go down lower, but most prefer to be invited to "come up higher." And yet, the Valley of Humiliation has a place in the life of every one. The most fertile soil is usually found down in the valley. There usually are to be found the tallest trees. And so it is in spiritual things. The man who lives constantly on the summit of prosperity and unadulterated happiness, is not calculated to be the best type of a christian. All sunshine would not develop a beautiful rose. Showers are needed to give color and fragrance. Like the flower, the character is best developed with both sunshine and showers, joy and sorrow, hills and valleys. Joseph was a much better man because of his experience down in the Valley of Humiliation. The pit and the prison hours were at the time most grievous, but in the end they all proved stepping stones to the throne of Egypt. To travel in this lonely valley of sorrow all alone, without the hand of the Lord to lead us, is to travel a most dismal road, and one where death would be preferable to life. But when the Lord is with the traveler, and His peace is his strength, then, all can be endured for Christ's sake, and the pilgrim goes on his way rejoicing, even unto death itself. When Louis XVI of France was on his way to execution, exposed to the most insulting clamor of the raging mob, he traveled through the very deepest valley of humiliation. When at the place of execution, the executioners came with cords to bind him to the plank, he most seriously objected. "No! no!" he exclaimed, "I will never submit to that, do your business, but you shall not bind me." When, however, the king turned to his confessor, as if for counsel, and was told by his spiritual adviser to submit to this fresh outrage, as the last resemblance to the Saviour who would soon recompense him for all his sufferings, Louis replied, "Assuredly there needed nothing less than the example of the Saviour to induce me to submit to such an indignity." Then reaching out his hands to his executioners he said, "Do as you will; I will drink the cup to the dregs." With such resignation in the valley of humiliation, we may well appreciate King Louis' words when he said, approaching the scaffold, "How happy am I that I maintained my christian faith while on the throne! What would have been my condition now, were it not for this hope?" It were indeed well for many to consider seriously the importance of having Christ as their Saviour while they are on the throne,—in health and prosperity, for when once they are led down into deep humiliation, then it often proves too late and man's eyes are opened to see the folly of the "foolish delights of youth." Take Christ along, and let come what may, go where you will, and His "rod and staff they comfort" thee.

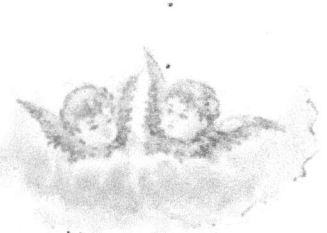

But Christian had scarcely reached the valley of humiliation before he spied, off in the distance, coming toward him, a most miserable looking fiend, which proved none other than Apollyon, the devil himself. It is rather strange that any one would be willing to be found in company with such a hateful looking fiend, and yet, the devil seems to win over to his companionship many choice followers. It is not strange however that those very followers are unwilling to confess that they are companions of the devil, for it is not much of a compliment to any one to be known as keeping company with such a repulsive looking creature. Notwithstanding all this, there are many who are daily walking in the very footsteps of Satan, fighting for him battles against the Lord and the church. It is truly painful to think of the bright promising young men and women who are in line with the evil one, and in refusing to become followers of Christ, they are in reality against Christ and for the adversary, for Christ has very distinctly said, "he that is not for me is against me." Even more than that, for He adds, "He that gathers not with me, scattereth." Later on a most dreadful conflict took place between

Christian and Apollyon.

When the fiend discovered he could not persuade Christian to turn back and become one of his followers, he dealt heavy blows upon him, until at length he overpowered him, and was about to give the last blow of death when Christian seized the sword which he had let fall in the struggle, and with it he drove off the enemy, and escaped with but a few bruises, which were afterward quickly healed by one who placed upon them leaves from the tree of life.

Bunyan's Christian, in his conflict with Apollyon in the Valley of Humiliation, is but typical of the conflict of many young men in the same valley. Discouragement, misfortune, failure have overtaken them, and for the time they feel humbled. In this hour of weakness Satan appears to them with all manner of offers which he is unable to fulfill. At such times of momentary weakness, many of the young yield and fall a prey to the enemy. Notwithstanding the fact, many of these very young men may have had good early training both at home and in the church, yet, perhaps away from home in a strange city among strangers, they are taken off their guard, and ere they are aware, in their conflict with sin and temptation, Satan gets the advantage over them, and like Christian of old, in the struggle the young man often lets his weapons of defense fall from his hands. Oh the awful conflicts that are being waged between the devil and many of our once promising and noble young men. Men who at one time were duly qualified to occupy places of honor and trust, where they might have been a blessing to the age in which they live. But alas for many such, they have yielded to temptation, they have sinned against the early teachings of their christian mothers. They have turned their back upon the church, and are being fleeced by the followers of the adversary, the devil, whose arrows are being hurled at them from various points of attack. Many indeed of the once strong young men are thus attacked and are under control of the enemy. Strong drink has taken hold of them with its cold iron grasp, that they are almost as helpless as babes, and while one by one of the poisoned arrows are being hurled at these men of promise, the very angels look down with pity, eagerly watching, and wishing to help them, lest the last deadly blow be given and all be over. While some of the young men are thus falling from strong drink, many others are being captured by evil associates. Little by little their poisonous influence is exerted upon the once innocent mind, until at last innocence is a thing of the past, and boldness in sin takes its place. If only our young could be convinced more and more of the evil influences of wicked companions! Not only are they judged by their associates, but many are corrupted by evil environments. Step by step they walk into the net spread by the enemy, until at last they are ensnared. In fact, our young people are not as wise as are birds; for when once birds have discovered that a net has been spread for them they keep far away from it. Conscious as every one must be that evil nets are spread, and as manifest as are many of such places, yet, with their eyes wide open, they walk into the very places where they know death awaits them, for "the wages of sin is death." Let a young man once lose his character, and he has lost his best friend and very passport into success, and a life of usefulness.

When in prison, Bunyan had sent to him a rosebush as a memorial of old friendship. At first he looked upon it with great admiration as do many at the first appearance of sin. The rose-bush later on grew a rose which attracted the lone prisoner more than ever. But when he went to pluck the rose it pricked his fingers. So it is with many of the sinful pleasures of life. At first they promise much, but when once they are plucked, then are discovered the hidden thorns, and many are left to go about with a wounded character and a saddened heart. The momentary gratification of sinful pleasures will not compensate for the lasting pangs of a guilty conscience, and many would gladly undo the past if it were only in their power to do so.

Some of the strongest men have fallen by the arrows of the evil one; even Peter, David, Solomon, Samson, and a host of mighty ones have been overcome by him that is ever "going about seeking whom he may devour." The misfortune with many is, they boast of their own strength, forgetting that others just as strong as themselves have yielded to temptation, and have had woven about them sinful habits, which at last bound them hand and foot, and robbed them of all that at one time was bright and hopeful. Could the secret history of many of the more unfortunate of life be known, it would be a tale of woe, and it would be discovered that sin was at the root, gnawing away the very sap of life and honorable success. God is accordingly blamed for much for which He is not responsible. Man has too often planted the thorn in his own pillow, for which he blames God. It was no fault of the Lord that the prodigal was clothed with rags, and assigned to a place among the swine. The young man paved his own way and walked in it, as a preference of his own choice. When once he landed at the wretched place, then his eyes were opened to the end of his journey, but it was too late. It were well if many could only see on ahead to the end of the path they are traveling, for seeing the wretched end, they would doubtless at once turn back and start life over again.

And yet, there is apparently no excuse for such, for they might well profit by the sad experiences of others who have gone on before them, and whose repeated trials dolefully signal all others from traveling that same way. Surely, youth should profit by the experiences of others, without wishing first to learn the "follies of youth" from their own personal experience.

Like Christian in "Pilgrim's Progress," such as are being tempted and attacked by the adversary, the devil, should quickly seize their sword, the Word of God, and with it put to flight the enemy, for the devil cannot argue against God's word, when that Word is properly used as the Sword of the Spirit. Unhappily many have sorely neglected the "Sword." At the time of their public profession of faith in God at the altar, they were, apparently, ready to use it on all occasions, like Peter when he cut off the ear of Malchus. But soon afterward the Sword, God's Word, is left fall into disuse, and like an unused sword becomes dusty and rusty. In fact, there are doubtless those who would have some little difficulty in finding the Sword, God's Word, for it has been so long since they used the same that they have forgotten when and where they last used it. Is it any wonder then that many of those who once professed the name of Jesus as their own Saviour, have since fallen away from grace and been conquered by the adversary, the devil? Such careless men in battle would soon be captured by the enemy, for offering no resistance. Nor can we expect such as call themselves soldiers of the cross of Christ, to resist temptation and sin, when they stand unguarded against the assaults of the devil. Rather let every one be watchful and stand fast in the faith, quitting themselves like men of God. With the Sword of the Spirit, they can resist the devil and he will flee from them, and they stand conquerors through Him that loved them and gave Himself for them.

CHAPTER V.

VALLEY OF DEATH AND BREAK OF DAY.

AFTER Christian's terrible conflict with Apollyon, and his triumph with the sword, he resumed his journey with "*Sword drawn in his hand*," for, said he, "I know not but some other enemy may be at hand.

This should be the attitude of every christian, the "sword drawn in hand," for the time to prepare for an enemy is not when once that enemy has laid his hand upon your shoulder, not when he has called upon you for a surrender, not when he has ensnared you in an evil net, but in the day of opportunity, in the day of your strength ; then is the time to prepare and be equipped for an attack. The builders of the wall under the instruction of their leader, Nehemiah, not only builded the wall, but stood ready and prepared at any moment for an assault from the enemy. They labored with one hand in the erecting of the wall, while in the other hand they held a sword to protect self. The children of Israel were commanded to eat the Passover "standing" so that at a moment's notice they might be ready for action at the call of God. The sentinel stands ever ready for an invasion. There is no time for hunting the rifle and loading it when once the enemy stands in front of you. So in spiritual matters. Too many are indifferent, and hence are taken unawares. Had David been on duty faithfully discharging the same, he would not have fallen into the net and been captured. It was during a period of idleness that the devil got hold of him, and like him, many others have been captured by Satan, because they were not sufficiently watchful. The devil always finds employment for idle persons, and especially, idle christians.

There is need of rekindling the fires upon the altar of many hearts that at one time were aglow for Christ, but since have become almost extinguished amid the ashes of indifference. Even the apostle Peter found the devil got hold of him when he was off duty; for when he stood idly by the fires of the enemy warming himself, then having denied his Master, the evil one laid hands upon him and claimed him as one of his own. Think of it! Peter, the apostle, denying his Saviour in the presence of a little servant girl, and later on cursing and swearing that he never knew Him! Alas! like him, many have since done likewise, if not in word at least in action, which speaks louder than words. Oh, christian man and woman, draw the sword for the cause of Christ, and march with "sword drawn in hand." lest unexpectedly the enemy meet you, and unguarded you fall! When once you have fallen, then the enemy has double chances over you, and your way will be all the more difficult to travel.

Nor was Christian mistaken in his expectation of meeting with enemies: very soon he found himself in the very midst of

"*The Valley of the Shadow of Death,*"

where he found two men retreating as fast as they possibly could, at the same time warning Christian against going on any farther in his journey, because of the dangers which beset the way. In this connection we are reminded of the spies sent out to survey the land of Canaan. They returned almost frightened out of their wits, saying they had seen men like giants, and that the land was very unhealthy, for, said they, "It eateth up the inhabitants." Poor fellows, scared over a few discouragements which they magnified to mountains, saying, "We will not go." The idea of six hundred thousand marshalled men being afraid to march up against a body of men who were neither armed nor united, for the Canaanites were scattered! But after all it is not so very strange, for even in this age of enlightenment and advancement, there are many like the spies and the men whom Christian found retreating in the valley of the shadow of death. A few troubles rise up before them, a few discouragements, and they at once become

alarmed and retire from the field of service, leaving all the battles to be fought by a few who stand loyally to their posts. If only such retreating ones would keep quiet, it would not be so bad, but dissatisfied themselves, they try to make others dissatisfied, and thus do double harm to Christ.

Oh, what would be the power of the church to-day if all who profess the name of Christ would be true to that profession! But, alas, many seem to forget what it means to be a christian in reality, rather than in mere sentiment! Too many are waiting for others to come and nurse them in their spiritual infirmities, without realizing the fact that they owe something to others, rather than to expect others to come forever and be doing for them. No christian man or woman has a right to expect others to do more for them than they are willing to do for others. Unhappily, many of the "Home Guard" are not only idly sitting there reading the reports of such as are in the front of the battle, enduring hardships as valiant soldiers of the cross of Christ, but they seem to think that those very ones who are doing all the hard fighting, should come to them and carry sweetmeats to tickle their palates. Why do not those very persons leave their places of ease and luxury, where nothing is being done by them, and go to the front and there offer their services, thus allowing others to be lightened of their heavy burdens? Surely it is as fair for one as for the other, and as God is no respecter of persons, unless such will march to the field of battle and offer their services, they surely cannot expect the same blessing from God when the day comes for the distribution of rewards. Don't, therefore, become discouraged because of a few stones of offence by the way, or because the way may at times lead through dark places, for after all, this is but a good sign that you are in the right way. No one has ever yet gotten to heaven "on flowery beds of ease," nor is there much likelihood that any ever will, so that such as are living with the expectation of escaping all trials, will be sorely mistaken. It is all folly to retreat because of discouragement. Some people seem to think they can be christians, and yet have the privilege at any time it pleases them to leave off the work of the Master and single out their own course and mode of living. If such were the teachings of

Christ then were it a most pitiable condition for the salvation of the world, for whenever the followers of Christ would become dissatisfied with the work, they could just quit and sit down and bask in the sunshine of the devil and his followers. These are the ones, who, like Peter, fall and are restored only by bitter tears of repentence, together with a future life of consecration to God and the church. Otherwise, they will share the fate of Judas who betrayed his Master, and afterward his soul was hurled into eternity, into darkness, into unspeakable anguish.

The spirit that should prompt every follower of God should be that of Christian when he said to such as would discourage him, "This is my way to the desired heaven." Unhappily, many of the discouraged christians listen to the idle words of the retreating. They seem to relish those things which injure the cause of Christ, and many are, unfortunately, only too ready to add fuel to the disheartened by encouraging them in their wrong thinking, when traveling through "the valley of the shadow of death," in which place the christian is sorely tested and even threatened with spiritual death. In that valley there are always to be found persons who, like the two men who met Christian, are ever ready to bear tidings that are utterly false and harmful. They are the servants of the devil carrying wicked messages. Instead of trying to make peace and thus help the cause of Christ and show the part of a true christian, many do just the opposite and do much harm. If such persons would stop for a moment and think of the results of their evil words, they would act very differently, for even after they are dead and gone, perhaps there will yet be growing the fruits of their evil sowing, and surely, there can be no satisfaction to any one for having been in-instrumental in causing trouble by their words. Why not be a peace-maker, and be loved because of the very fragrance of your words which make peace!

In this valley, Christian had another peculiar experience, for soon he came to a place where there was

'a deep pit,'

and from it came forth both flames and smoke, and near by were many snares and pitfalls

This is but another of the many experiences along the way of life. You will not be able to travel very far toward the Celestial City, before you meet with these very experiences. Because he was unmindful to the call of God, Jonah learned to know the agonies of the deep pit. David wept and "his bones waxed old" amid his groanings and moanings day and night, because of his transgressions. There are many pitfalls carefully prepared for the capture of young men and women. The devil loves a shining mark, and hence he aims at the youth of the land. He is not satisfied merely with the old and dying, but delights in the capture of the young, so that he may have an army of strong, active persons to serve him. In our young people lies great strength for good or evil. Would to God that noble power were consecrated to God and the church! What work might be accomplished for the salvation of the world, and the betterment of society, and mankind! What happy homes would be the result! What fathers and mothers would rejoice instead of weep over the conduct of their children!

Bad literature, has proven a pitfall for many of our youth. Books and papers which tend to shatter the faith of the religious, should be consigned to the flames, for they rob man of all, and give him nothing in return, but the ashes of a wrecked faith. Once outside the fold of Christ, the young are exposed to the snares of the devil, and have but little show for safety. Let a young man try to live independent of the church and he will find very serious dangers besetting his way and ere he is aware, he is a captive in one of the pitfalls of the enemy. Much of the literature of to-day is demoralizing in its tendency, and corrupts the minds of the young, undermining their faith in Christ. Indeed many of the novels are not fit for a place in the home, and are mental alcohol to the reader.

The dance as it is carried on in many places, is another most dangerous pitfall for our youth. Dangerous for two reasons. First, to the body. Many young persons have impaired their health, gone into hasty decline, and to an untimely grave because of the dance.

I question very much whether or not parents are not to blame in many instances for these untimely deaths, for the child is educated for the dance, and thereafter it is but natural for the child to put

 into practice that which it has been taught. Then, too, there is another danger that often results from the dance, and that is the moral danger. Public balls and promiscuous dancing, where the young are indiscriminately thrown in the arms and embrace of each other, is not, generally speaking, very conducive to morals. Many enter such circles where there are persons that a lady would not want to entertain in her parlor. And yet, at the public ball she is carried around in the arms of one of such. A woman's dance once cost the head of one of the very best men that ever lived, John the Baptist. That young woman was not the only one who sacrificed a life for the dance, for some have lost even more than life: they have lost a soul. It is well, therefore, for our youth to think well of some of the hidden pitfalls that lie before them, lest their eyes be opened when too late.

Why do I plead for our youth? I plead for them because of the dangers that lie before them. I plead for them because of their influence and power in the world. I plead for them because, when robbed of all, the world will do nothing more for them but cast them aside, friendless and hopeless. I plead for the young because I love them for their souls' sake. I plead for them because I want them to be truly happy and successful in life. And I plead for them because I want them at last to share the reward of the righteous in glory above. Young men and women, I plead for you "that you may prosper even as your soul prospers," and that at last you may receive the plaudit, "Well done, thou good and faithful servant, enter thou into the joys of thy Lord."

Happy for Christian, indeed, was the fact that at last there came for him

"*the break of day.*"

Such cheerless valleys have an end, and sooner or later the Lord opens up before the pilgrim a way of escape from the trials and temptations that beset him. Christian, therefore, could well be delighted and say, "He hath turned the shadow of death into morning." And so there is the break of day to every christian, a passing from the night and valley of sin out into the open plain and dawn of the liberty of the children of God. Once Christian thought if only he had a new heart, then would he hate sin, and be free from all evil, but there are times when the darkness seems to come back upon the soul, and for the time the traveler apparently gropes for his way in " the valley of the shadow of death." Like St. Paul he finds " a law in his members warring against the law of his mind; the flesh lusteth against the spirit, and the spirit against the flesh." Faith thus struggles with sin and doubt, each one striving for the mastery. Many christians have thus experienced times when the battle with sin was dark and heavy. Although man loves God, and knows the power of Christ, yet, he observes some sad deficiencies, which hang like shadows and clouds over his soul. But like Christian, he bethinks himself of the weapon of prayer, and kneeling down before God, he prays in all fervency, laying hold of the promises of Christ, clinging to the Saviour until he has been blessed. The darkness now becomes absorbed by the morning light, and the crooked things are made straight. A moment before, Christian sank: now, the break of day has come to his soul, and he sings for joy. The overshadowing clouds of doubt and sin have been rolled away, and he beholds the 'break of day of God's love in his heart. Many a man and woman have thus gone on in sin until at last the light from heaven has shone round about them, and, like Paul of old, the soul awoke to the divine light, and the old man was put off and the new man Christ Jesus put on, so that henceforth they could say, "Not I, but Christ liveth in me."

It may seem to some that they can never get out of the " valley ;" but let all such remember that the same road that leads *to* the valley, leads *through* the valley, on to the ridge of the break of day. Often in temporal affairs we are ushered down into the very " valley of the shadow of death," when it would seem all had been swept away from us. Only gloom and despair stare us in the face, and often at such times death would almost seem preferable. But " why art thou cast down, oh my soul, and why art thou disquieted within me? Hope thou in God, and He will bring all things to pass," that "shall work together for good to them that love Him." At the very time when we least expect, often the day breaks and the morning light and joy come. There are times when the "valley" seems so long and dark that it would appear there is no end to the night, but God is holding the reins of the universe. God reigneth, and slumbers neither day nor night! The trouble with many is they are trying to pass through "the valley" wholly in their own strength, without asking for the help of God. Wherefore, seize the weapon of prayer and use it wisely! It is not always an easy thing to pray, and many use this part of christian armor unwisely. We should pray like Jacob did when he said to the angel with whom he had been wrestling all night, "I will not let thee go except thou bless me." Too many pray formally, or when they are half asleep, and were God to answer their prayer, they would, indeed, be taken unawares, for they expect not that for which they ask, and hence do not receive it. We should also pray as did blind Bartimeus when he said, "Lord, that I may receive my sight." That prayer came from the very depth of his soul, and he was sincerely in earnest. He wanted his sight, and the Lord granted his request. Many are blind spiritually, and were they to ask God in the spirit of Bartimeus for spiritual vision, they would receive their sight. We should also pray as did Peter, when he found himself sinking. A large wave came rolling along carrying him deep down out of sight of Christ, who came walking to him on the sea. At once, therefore, Peter realized his utter helplessness and begged the Lord to help him, saying, "Lord, save, I perish." The great trouble with many, both in their sins and in their afflictions, is they first try all manner of other remedies, instead of coming and throwing themselves wholly into the arms of faith and the Lord in prayer. But the best prayer of all is that which Christ Himself prayed: "Father—thy will be done." We are too prone to pray selfishly, and ask God to give regardless of that which is best for us. Better pray God to make us solely humble and submissive to His will, that we may do whatsoever He would have us do; that we would go wheresoever He would have us go; and that we would submit to whatsoever

He would have us submit. "Not my will, but thine be done, O Lord," should be the spirit of all our prayers. Then shall we most reasonably expect an answer to our prayers, and "the break of day will be sure to come." God has placed many in the "valley," in order that they might be brought to the true light as it is in Christ Jesus, causing the soul to rejoice, saying, "Joy cometh in the morning."

CHAPTER VI.
VANITY FAIR.

CHRISTIAN doubtless realized the fact that by laying down the burden of the world, he had taken up the cross of Christ, for there were not many days along his journey when he did not have some experience of cross-bearing. In fact that is only the natural indication of being a follower of Christ, for without the cross for the Master, no one can be His disciple. "Whosoever will not deny himself," says Christ, "and take up his cross and follow me, is not worthy of being my disciple."

It is a mistaken idea to suppose we are to escape all cross-bearing, when Christ Himself bore the cross for the sins of the world, and surely we are not to expect to get to heaven by any other way than that of following in the footsteps of Him who has gone on before us. Lest Christian might, perchance, forget this fact, Evangelist appeared to him again, and not only encouraged him for his success in the past, but also admonished him to be careful in the future, for, said Evangelist to Christian, "You are not yet out of

the gunshot of the devil."

Like Christian we all need to be forcibly reminded of this warning, for too often we boast of our safety and think we are at a vantage ground where we can be sure of standing. Many have thus boasted only to see the very foundation fall, on which their hopes were built. Boastfulness begets vanity and personal pride, which so undermines faith in Christ that man is sure to fall, sooner or later. It is always well to be conscious of personal weakness and a longing to be stronger in the faith of our Lord Jesus Christ. Leaning on one's own understanding, is but leaning upon a broken reed.

"Come just this one time, do just this one act, drink just this one glass." It all sounds very innocent, and to many seems harmless, but the one act, the one glass, has often opened the very floodgates, into which rushed the river like a mighty torrent, carrying along everything before it to ruin and destruction. Many have thus been innocently captured by the tempter, and fallen a prey into the hands of the enemy of sinful habits. "You are not yet out of the gunshot of the devil," and to think self safe may be to fall into the wiles of the adversary.

It is "dangerous to slack up in the race;" for often the delay proves most disastrous. King Louis Sixteenth of France, during the time of his flight, would have escaped, had not his carriage broken down. That delay of half an hour, however, proved fatal, and he was captured by the enemy. Many others in a spiritual sense have lost a half hour by the way. That time is gone forever, but the results of such a loss still remain, and the delay along the journey of life by such occasions, has resulted in the downfall of many who at one time seemed sure of safety. The crown is at the goal, and unless we are persevering unto the very end of the journey, we cannot expect the reward of the faithful. The Bible needs to be read just as faithful ten years after the start in the christian race, as at the beginning of that race. Prayer is as important twenty years after the peace of God came into the heart as it was at the very start of christian experience. Worship of God is as essential to the healthy in body thirty years after the confession of Christ as Saviour, as it was at the time that profession was made. There is no spare time in holy living.

Christians need to be as faithful to their trust, as the clock is to time. The pendulum might complain of the constant toil and swing. It might get tired of the monotony of swinging to and fro, hour after hour, and day after day. It has no time to itself, but must constantly be on the go. In a sense it might appear to be accomplishing but very little; merely moving back and forward in the same space over the same territory, day in and day out. It has no chance for a

change. And yet, that swinging pendulum is faithfully discharging its duty, keeping the clock in motion and the correct time is given to every passer by. The clock itself might reasonably offer up a lot of complaints, for being constantly shelved, while day after day it is wound up merely to run over the same line of work, year in and year out. Yet, the wheels revolve, and the cog within moves, each part performing its several functions.

Christians will do well to pattern after the clock, and not grow weary in well doing. It is all folly to start well and then stop. Better never have started at all, than to fail in the end, for "to him that knoweth to do good and doeth it not, to him it is sin." We need to be as faithful and regular at our post as the pendulum is in the discharge of its duty.

Christian was admonished to "set his face like a flint," and were more thus firmly fixed in "the faith," there would be less to murmur or complain. Because you may have done well in the past, is no argument for laziness in the future. The pendulum is not excused from action because at one time it did its work well. The faithful swinging in the past is but the better recommendation for its future truthfulness. So christians who have been most faithful in the past, are expected to be all the more faithful in the future. Never leave the safe vessel for an old rotten boat. The fact that the ship has proven safe in the time of storm, is the best proof in favor of remaining on board that vessel. Only an insane man would leave a safe steamer for an old rotten barge. Spiritually speaking, this is even more true. Christ is the only firm foundation, and such as would leave Christ and go aboard the rotten ship of the world, will find as did Jehoshephat that at the very time when they expect to go to Ophir for gold, that an unexpected storm will have arisen and the ships be broken. Of them it will be said as it was of Jehoshephat, "They went not, because their ships were broken."

It were indeed well if christians would pattern in some respects after the men and women who are members of the various orders, societies, and lodges. In these various associations the members do not complain when asked to do anything, but simply do it. When their dues are payable, there is no complaint as regards the payment of the same, but the money is laid down without any question. All is apparently done cheerfully and largely. But this kind of spirit is frequently wanting in the work of the church. While it might be comparatively easy to contribute a few dollars as dues to a society, that same amount given to the cause of Christ would be deemed by many christians, a very great sacrifice. To attend the various meetings of such orders is regarded a pleasure, and no complaints are offered, whether it be cold or hot, whether it be moonlight or rain, whether it be near or far. But when it comes to a question of the church with many such, they are like the one of old, and say, " I pray thee have me excused." Or if it be an appeal for missions or other needs of the church, they will hunt up a few rusty pennies that happen to be left over from payment for things of the world, the flesh and the devil. Such need to be on their guard, for they "are not yet out of the gunshot of the devil."

Like Christian of old, they are often made to realize the force of such a warning, for ere they are aware, they find themselves in the very midst of

" *Vanity Fair.*"

This is indeed a very old town, and many have passed within its tempting streets, only to be lured by siren voices, and be captured by the tempter. The merchandise of this "fair" is such as is common in every village, town or city. Even Christ Himself was accosted on the lonely mountain by one from this "fair" who was eager to sell his ware, for the devil had the presumption to tempt Christ shortly after the Master's baptism. That same tempter has been at it ever since, and has sold much of his goods, for not all are wise as was Christ, who refused to buy but said, "Get thee behind me Satan." Many have entered this fair of vanities, with great riches of health, wealth and character. But alas, not a few of those very same persons have come away from "vanity fair" paupers, for while at the devil's booth all things are sold, yet "each ounce of dross costs its ounce of gold." Health is often destroyed by feeding upon the unwholesome food secured at "the fair." The sinner soon discovers that the ways of the world are not conducive to a healthy frame of either body or mind. Gradually the nervous system is destroyed, and healthy muscles burned up, until at last there stands but the skeleton of what was at one time a healthy body. As with the health, so with riches. Money is soon spent in "vanity fair." A few dollars do not last long at that place, nor do they purchase much. Before man knows it, he is robbed of his hard earnings. Many today are living in squalor and pauperism, who at one time possessed all that was necessary for a comfortable livelihood, but entering "vanity fair," indulging in the follies of life, "eating, drinking, and being merry," they soon spent their all and there "arose a mighty famine" in their life's experience. Such persons have no one to blame but themselves. They allowed themselves to be fleeced until at last they were robbed of all their money and their backs clothed with rags, while their table was wanting the necessaries of life. Thus, the devil gets the home and gives man instead the hovel. The devil takes the fatted calf and gives man the ashes.

With health and wealth, many have sold their character at "vanity fair." Robbed of health and wealth, character is man's best friend, but when once character is gone, then man is a miserable wreck. Men and women may be ever so humble, yet, if they be honorable they have riches worthy of high esteem and confidence. But let them lose the God-given principle of character, and they are robbed of all that makes life worth living. Alas! how many lose this very thing in "vanity fair!" They want to see the world. They are anxious to know something more about life, than that which is learned in the home from parents. They want to see for themselves the doings of the world. They enter the "fair" for themselves. But through such experiences, many have afterward left the ways of the world to find themselves robbed of their very best possession, character.

With character they also lose friends in "vanity fair." Let those whom sin has fleeced count up their friends and see how very few they have. No need of using the fingers of both hands for such a count, for they will not be able to find enough for the fingers of one hand. So long as you feast, your halls will be crowded, but when once your feasts are all over then the world will pass you by unnoticed. Many a man has gone on in the world thinking he had a

 host of friends, but discovered when too late, that he had none, save such as were using him for what they could get out of him. Open up your halls of feasting again, and soon you will have back all of your old acquaintances. Such is the way of the world, and a man is a fool who will see these things, and yet keep on squandering his money in "vanity fair." Unfortunately, it is true of many, that while experience is a dear teacher, "yet, fools will not learn in any other way."

Christian found at the ",Fair " some very disreputable characters, and such as were dangerous to touch, for among them were "cheats, rogues and thieves." How like many at the present day who bring forward their wares and try to tempt our young men and women to purchase! The inexperienced see only the coating, they taste only the sugar, and in their innocency, they are blind to the hidden poison; the deadly hook is covered up by the tempting bait. It is very true of many of the young that they are "as fishes of the sea." The bait is dropped down before them and without thought they bite and the work is done.

It were well if men and women would profit by the unhappy experiences of the unfortunate, and seeing wherein others have erred and been deceived, guard against those very things whereby others fell. Don't taste poison for the sake of knowing how it tastes.

"You are the first one to tell me of my faults, others have flattered me," said a gentleman one afternoon, "but," he added, "the flatterer is not my friend." For this reason "we warn men" because we love them.

At "vanity fair," Bunyan's Christian was characterized in three different ways from the rest of the people at the "fair."

First of all, "he was clothed differently." Like him, christians should be different from the world. Not fanatical, but a look that will show to the world "that they have been with Jesus and learned of him." Too many christians are hanging on to their "grave clothes," refusing to "put off" entirely, "the old man" of sin for "the new man Christ Jesus." Some have a "Sunday suit" and a "week-day suit," trying thus to "serve both God *and* mammon." The soldier is known by the clothes he wears as to the side on which he is fighting. And so christians are to be sufficiently marked that it may be discerned on which side they are fighting, whether for or against the Lord. If you saw a man lying drunk along the street it would not be difficult to tell on which side he was fighting. If on the other hand you saw a man going about doing good to the sick and needy, you would at once be able to tell on which side that man was fighting. "By their fruits ye shall know them." for "men do not gather grapes from thorns nor figs from thistles."

Christian was also known by "his speech." Much of the conversation is utterly demoralizing. It is indeed alarming to hear much of the conversation that falls from the lips of many of the present day. Even in the parlor, the conversation is frequently not of that real refining character that it should be, and it were well in many instances if the parlor doors could be swung wide open, and the parent be present as a purifier of that which is said. There is no doubt but that the parlor is frequently abused, and that too in ways without number. One very common mistake is to drive the sons out of the parlor for fear they may disarrange some of the ornaments, or destroy the furniture. Far better to allow them to use the parlor than to drive them out into the streets. Better allow the son to entertain his friends in the parlor than for him to meet them on the street corners. Could many of the young men of to-day speak, they would be able to tell of the harmful results in being compelled to entertain their friends on the street, instead of welcoming them in the home parlor. The home should be made so attractive that the very parlor itself would eclipse all desire for the "vanity fairs" of the world. Men will have associates and if they cannot receive their friends in the home they will go out in the world and form acquaintances. Better allow some of the furniture to be even broken by the sons, than drive them away from home for enjoyment, for sons that are properly reared in the home, in after days will be able to repay a dozen times all they destroyed when boys. Besides, such sons will be an honor to their parents, as well as a great source of gratification and assistance. Among the birthday gifts which may be given a son when he is twenty-one years of age, is a 'Night Key.' But unfortunately for many sons they receive that gift when too young. The mother who sits up at night to open the door for the return of her son or daughter, is much wiser than the mother who gives the son and daughter a 'night key,' to return at their own pleasure, at any hour of the night. Sad, indeed, is it for those sons and daughters who, through death, have no mother to thus counsel them, for after years often tell very forcibly what has been lost by such denials. Be careful in the selection of your companions, and associate only with such as have purity of speech, ever remembering that "your conversation is in heaven." Hence, "let your conversation be as becometh the gospel of Jesus Christ." " Let no corrupt communication proceed out of your mouth," but rather "speak that which is good to the use of edifying."

The third characteristic of Christian in "vanity fair" was he had "little regard for their wares." All manner of articles were offered him, but when tempted he would silently pray saying, "Turn away mine eyes from beholding vanity." It is a sad fact that many do just the very opposite, for instead of praying that they might not see vanity they go forth in search of it. In our large cities there is much that is ennobling, and many are the opportunities for self-culture and success in life. But, instead, many go forth in search of that which is low and debasing. They see "apples of Sodom" and at once stop and price them. Sugar-coated, as are all such offers of the devil, many taste, eat and fall. It is dangerous to barter with the devil, for when once a conversation is entered into then Satan gets a strong foothold, and in the end often carries off his booty. Better by far to have nothing to do with the "wares" of the devil, and when tempted, do as did Christian ; silently pray to God saying, "Turn away mine eyes from beholding vanity."

CHAPTER VII.
"BUY THE TRUTH."

To be a true follower of the Lord Jesus Christ, means more than a mere negative attribute. It is not enough for one to "cease to do evil." If that were all the Lord required of His followers, then it would be an easy matter to be a christian. It would be about as cheap as many seem to wish religion were. One of the great problems of the present day, that is puzzling the minds of many, is to know just how little is required of them to get to heaven. They are willing to cease doing evil, but are unwilling to put into practice the second requirement, or, the "doing good" part of religion. It was therefore only natural for the people at "Vanity Fair" to ask of Christian "what he would buy," since he refused to buy or even price their wares. They seemed to say to him, "Sir, if you refuse to buy our goods,

'what will ye buy?'"

It is so with every one. Man must decide one way or the other. If you are *against* a certain matter or person, you must surely be *for* something else or for some other person. You are *something*. If you are not one thing, you are surely another. Otherwise you would be like the painted Jackdaw. It disliked its own kind, and to be different from them, it was painted white. Seeing some doves fly by, the painted jackdaw joined them. But no sooner had the jackdaw opened his mouth than the doves discovered him to be a traitor and not one of their number, and at once unmercifully drove him away. He then decided to go back again to his old company, but the jackdaws didn't like his looks, and refused to have anything to do with him, and so, the poor painted bird had no where to go, for he was neither a dove nor a jackdaw. This is the unfortunate condition of some professing christians; they are not wanted among the true followers of God because their speech betrays them, nor are they wanted among the people of the world, because they dislike a hypocrite, and as a result, they are a sort of Mahomet's coffin, suspended between heaven and earth.

If any one wants to be a true follower of God, he must "follow" and not stand still. He must "buy" something. He must "do something." Otherwise he will be like the man who each morning went down to the saw-mill and polished the saw, put all in readiness, greased all the parts of the machinery, saw that everything was in good order, but he never did any work. He had all in readiness, but never a log was sawed. There, month after month, the mill stood ready, and yet, it stood idle. The christian who stands ready like the mill, but never does anything, might just as well not be ready. Better even not to make such a profession, for it only deceives others. Christ Himself dislikes deception, for when He saw the fig tree green, looking as if it were laden down with fruit, but upon examination saw that the tree was barren, having on it "nothing but leaves," the Lord was displeased and cursed the tree, that it died. Better make no profession at all than make one and be untrue to it, for deception not only imposes upon but displeases God.

When, therefore, Christian was asked, "What will you buy?" he did not endeavor to explain away his faith, by trying to carry water on both shoulders, but he was true enough to stand by his colors, and stand boldly on the Lord's side. Hence, he said, "We buy the truth." This at once told the people just where he stood. There was no question about his belief; no dallying with the world, but a bold declaration of his faith in that which was right. He wanted the "Truth" and nothing else would answer.

"We buy the truth," should be the motto of every follower of God, for without the "Truth" there can be no sanctification. "Sanctify them by thy truth," and the "Truth" that best sanctifies is God's Holy Word, the Bible.

People are always gathering information, and there is a great

tendency to gather much that is most undesirable. Evil gossip is a thing easily to be secured, "without money and without price." In fact, it is thrust into your very face. Gossip, like bad literature, is very cheap and plentiful. There is much said that would better never have been uttered, and it is a dangerous thing to listen to and believe all that is spoken. It were well, indeed, if people would "buy the truth" and not take "without cost" everything that is offered them. Chaff is very cheap, and easily carried about. Much of the damaging talk is like chaff, so very light that little effort is required to scatter it broadcast over the land. We do well, accordingly, to discount much that we hear, and make an effort to get at the truth. It may not always be easy, yet, it is the proper thing. "Buy the truth."

Buy it at any price, for the truth and only the truth is worth possessing. The truth is cheap at any price, while evil gossip is expensive even when received without any cost. Very little of the real truth is acquired without a price. The young man who wishes to become a physician must pay for the truth. The apprentice does not get the truth of his calling for nothing, but must pay for what he gets. The client desirous of the truth is required to buy it from legal authorities before he gains possession of the same. The patient before he gets the truth from his physician, is expected to pay for the cure, or the truth. We must " buy the truth."

But while we must " buy the truth " it is also a fact that, the
truth often causes a " hubbub."

Just as soon as it was discovered at "Vanity Fair" that Christian was a purchaser only of the "truth," then at once the people were opposed to him. He and his friend "Faithful," who had been with him for some time, were mocked and bound with chains, and thus weighted down, they were driven through the streets as a terror and warning to any others who might be desirous of becoming followers of Christ with Christian and Faithful.

This seems to be the nature of "Truth;" it often arouses animosities on the part of those of the world. St. Paul at Ephesus soon discovered that upon the preaching of the "Truth," people became incensed, and at once were up in arms against him. The result was a terrible "uproar and tumult" at Ephesus. Wrong doing cannot stand the truth, for it tells a man just what he is, and often people don't like others to know those things, nor do they like to be reminded of their faults. When the shoe fits too closely, the wearer is apt to offer some complaint. It is a truth in such instances that the "shoe fits," and hence the wearer recognizes the application. The trouble with some persons is, they are like the passenger on board a steamer. He was upbraiding the captain, and calling him all manner of ugly names, when the captain, very politely turned the "other cheek" and gave the passenger a blow upon his own cheek, which at certain times seems to be the gospel idea of "turning the other cheek." At once the passenger cried out, "I'm tender." Like him, many say all manner of things about others, and in their very life do much that is to the harm of their fellowmen, their wives and children; but as soon as the "truth" is declared, it causes a "hubbub" and they become very much offended, saying, "I'm tender." Alas! If the church must keep quiet on certain lines for fear of hurting some one's feelings, then it might as well close its doors, and let the devil take charge of things. "I'm tender." Yes, it were well if some persons were a little more tender, and in their dealings with mankind they would consider "the other fellow," as well as their own selfish ends. You owe something to your neighbor as well as to yourself, and no one has a right to do that which will injure his neighbor, unless thereby he accomplish greater results and blessings to a greater number of individuals, and in all God be glorified. "Am I my brother's keeper?" Yes, you are your brother's keeper, and as such, you owe him a brother's part. You cannot afford to bury the truth for the sake of pleasing the devil or even his followers. That is just what the devil has been after since his fall. He is trying to bury truth, and then he would be king on the throne. It would not be long, under such a rule, before we would fall back into the customs of the "dark ages," when we would have "the survival of the fittest." Brute force would then be the power to rule, and our sons and daughters would not be safe on the streets, even in broad daylight.

"The fear of man bringeth a snare," and if the christian wants to pass through life without ever incurring the displeasure of the world, he will have a hard time getting to heaven. Better be on the Lord's side and be popular with Him, than have the good will of some one of the world. "Buy the truth," even though it cost the "enmity of the world."

Not only does the "truth" often cause a "hubbub," but there are also

"*False Witnesses Against the Truth.*"

Soon there were three witnesses, "Envy, Superstition and Pickthank," who came forward to bear false testimony against Christian. These three men had each been grieved by what Christian had said about their mode of living. They didn't like him to tell them the truth, and just as soon as an opportunity afforded, they were ready to bear false witness against him. These three men have many children. When King Ahab wanted to get Naboth out of the way, he employed the services of false witnesses. False witnesses were soon ready to report on duty for casting Daniel into the lion's den. Just as soon as it was discovered that the three Hebrew children did not bow the knee at the call of Nebuchadnezzar, there were busy bodies to quickly run and report to the ruler the fact. It required but very little trouble to find false witnesses to testify against Christ. There are plenty of persons who regard their word as of little consequence, and are ever ready to offer their services as "false witnesses." The world has in it many ready wicked messengers, who find great pleasure in collecting and distributing evil reports. Some of the false witnesses against Christian were prompted by "Envy," and were the truth known, it would be discovered that in most cases, envy lies at the bottom of the evil reports. But, "false witnesses" are punished sooner or later. The falsehood of Jezebel against Naboth led to her being devoured by the dogs in the street where she had Naboth put to death. Chickens come home to roost, and many a treacherous Judas, has lived to sorely regret his deceit and meanness Surely, "the way of the transgressor is hard," and especially with "false witnesses."

But a few false witnesses cannot stop the preaching of Truth.

"Faithful" died in bearing testimony to the truth, but at once "Hopeful" rose up out of the very ashes of his fallen predecessor, and became a companion with Christian in his pilgrimage.

Truth is not dependent upon one witness. Moses was a great leader, and yet, his death did not keep others from entering Canaan. Neither an Elijah nor an Elisha held the reins of the heavenly steed that carried Truth to the world and mankind. Noah and Enoch might walk with God, and yet, when once they ceased to walk with Him because of their departure to a better land, that did not leave God alone, for there were others to rise up and "walk with Him." Polycarp might be burned at the stake and Blandina be cast into the awful pit, but out of their very ashes rose up others to bear testimony to the truth. The Great Teacher, "Who spake as never man spake," was cut down as the great Vine, and yet, the truth did not die out, for there were other branches to spring forth from the true Vine. The Apostles might all be put to death in an unnatural manner, but the truth could not be wiped out of existence.

The death of martyrs only kindled the flames to cause the truth to shine forth all the more brilliantly. When once the light has gone forth from the sun you can't stop it. You may build high walls, you may shut yourself up in a dark cell, yet, the light is all the while shining, and no sooner is there a very small crevice, than the light at once creeps in and introduces itself. And so it is with the divine light of Truth. Christ is not only the "Way," but He is also the "Truth and the Light."

Neither is any one individual nor class of individuals able to extinguish that light. The nailing of Christ to the cross did not extinguish the light of the Truth, but rather spread abroad all the more that light, for the Cross of Christ has become that power of salvation, that, "all the light of sacred story, gathers round its head sublime," and from all parts of the world the Macedonian cry is being heard, "Come over and help us!" At the death of our great Reformers, doubtless many thought the work would be crippled But, although mighty men have fallen, yet, the work goes on in the name of the Lord, to the upbuilding of the Church of God.

One blessed thought for such as "buy the truth," is that before them is something that repays them for the difficulties they may have to encounter in the purchase of the same. Although Christian was compelled to walk about the "fair" weighted down with heavy chains for sport to the people; and although he was beaten and afterward "caged," yet, in all these things he could say with Paul, "The light afflictions of the present worketh for me a far more exceeding and eternal weight of glory." Yes, he could say, "I reckon that the sufferings of the present are not worthy to be compared with the glory that shall be revealed in me," and it was not long afterward that he obtained a glimpse of what God had in store for him at the end of his journey.

Although he was soon accosted by one named "By-ends" who tried to persuade him to change his course, yet Christian could not be influenced. True, the religion of "By-ends" was very tempting, for said he to Christian, "'Tis true we differ somewhat in religion from those of the stricter sort, yet, but in two small points: First, we never strive against wind and tide. Secondly, we are always most zealous when Religion goes in his silver slippers." Yes, that would be a very easy religion to live. No trouble about battling against sin, but merely allowing the enemy without interruption to go on and do as he pleased. Then, too, it meant to get money in any way possible, no matter how it had been secured, and then allow that sort of money to speak and rule. The religion was in the "silver slipper" and, therefore, not very strict. By-ends, offered a religion that is most pleasing to many in other respects, for instead of rushing on in his journey in all kinds of weather, he would wait for the tide and wind to carry him along without effort. Then, too, he would not travel when the roads were muddy or rough, for "he walks in his silver slippers," and would, therefore, travel only in the sunshine and with applause.

Don't have a "silver slipper religion"
which takes you out in the Master's service only when the tide is in your favor, and when the road is smooth and the weather fair. With that sort of religion you will not make much progress along the way of the Lord. If you worship God only on clear Sundays, and go to

church only when "the tide is in your favor," or rather when you "feel like going," then you will find the devil getting in very good work, so far as your religion is concerned. Many, indeed, are the moral wrecks lying now along the shores of Time, because they did that which was right only when "the tide and wind" were in their favor, or when the weather was favorable to "silver slipper religion."

Far better to soil the "slipper" than to neglect the soul in absenting one's self from the place of worship because the weather may happen to be just a little inclement. The weather never effects "silver slippers" when the wearer of the same wants to attend any worldly pleasures. No matter how cold the night, or how rainy the evening, it is then not a matter of "silver slippers" but of desire to go. Surely, christian men and women should have at least as much devotion to their God as the men and women of the world have for "the things which perish!" Christian, therefore, very wisely refused to listen to any such pleas, and quickened his steps, lest the tempter might lure him away from the right path, the way of Truth. As a result of his devotion to the right cause, he soon found his way leading to a most pleasant river, which David the king called, "the river of God;" but John, "the river of the water of life." Here Christian found things most delightful, for never before had he seen such a lovely place. Not only did they drink of the waters, but on either side of the river, were green trees with all kinds of fruit. The christian who is truly devoted to his faith in Christ will thus be brought into many places of soul refreshment, where the "weary and heavy laden find rest unto their souls." And, too, when resting in places where the Lord leads us, we are perfectly safe, for he gives his angels charge over us.

True, Satin is almost everywhere watching for an opportunity to do mischief, and yet, he has very little opportunity to do it among those who gather "together in heavenly places in Christ Jesus." He may be able to look in through the keyhole or through the windows, but such as are "pure in heart" are buyers only of the Truth. Such are safe in the presence of Jesus, and "he maketh them to lie down in green pastures beside the river of the waters of life."

CHAPTER VIII.
DOUBTING CASTLE.

THERE are times apparently, in the experiences of all christians when they for the time become dissatisfied with their way, and are ready to make a change for that which appears better.

It was thus with Christian and Hopeful. They were much disheartened because of the way. So it was with the children of Israel. As they journeyed from Mount Hor by way of the Red Sea, to compass the land of Edom, the "soul of the people was much discouraged because of the way." Their discouragement led to their complaint, as is often the case. Accordingly they indignantly asked of their leader, Moses, saying, "Wherefore have ye brought us up out of Egypt to die in the wilderness?"

It is wrong to complain and murmur against the ways of God, for it shows a lack of confidence in His ways, and for this want of faith and confidence, God sometimes punishes, as when He "sent fiery serpents among the people, which bit many."

Like Israel the Pilgrims "wished for a better way." As, therefore, they went on in their journey, they saw on the side of the road a meadow, and over the fence a stile leading to it. This was a temptation to the weary pilgrims, for the meadow looked so much more inviting than the rough road they had been traveling. Hence Christian said to his companion, "Let us go over into the meadow."

No sooner had they crossed over than they saw before them a path. This path seemed to lay along side the way in which they had been traveling, and so they thought themselves perfectly safe in walking along the path since it was so much smoother than the rough way. As they walked along "they found it very easy to their feet."

How like the experience of many others in life. The devil always prepares a stile leading into "By-path-meadows," and when once he succeds in getting christian men and women to depart from the right path he points them to a road that apparently lies just along-side the right way, and many are tempted, and blindly follow him. At first, they find the way, "easy to their feet," for the beginning of sin is very pleasant. It is, indeed, not only inviting but tempting, and many step aside because of the seeming happy change. Many, alas, have said, "Come, here is the easiest going!" But the end thereof is destruction. Christian even saw a man going on before them, "Vain Confidence," who invited them on, telling them they were in the right way that led to the Celestial City, but as night came on and it grew dark, suddenly the man before them disappeared and they were left alone. They looked for and called to the man, and at last, they saw a deep pit before them into which "Vain-Confidence" had fallen. It was a pit made by the prince of those grounds to catch "vain-glorious fools." Many have had similar experiences. They have followed some one who has offered them an easy way to heaven, only to perish in the end. Some people object to the plain Gospel, and want some other way of getting to heaven than that of the "strict way." Accordingly they find another way in which they travel. "Vain-Confidence" leads them on for a time, but before such get to heaven they find "pits" prepared for them. Far better to travel the rough way, the way of self-denial and sacrifice, than the "smooth way" and lose all in the end. Never follow a leader who promises you "smooth sailing" to heaven, for you will be disappointed. Rather follow that leader who tells you of your faults, and who urges you to a more holy life.

Many who have sought an "easy way" have afterward been compelled to repent saying, "Oh, that I had kept on my way!" Like Christian, they say in seeming surprise, "Who could have thought that this path should have led us out of the way!"

But now came the sad part of the story. The departure was easy enough, but the return to the right way was not so easy. It

was dark, and a flood had arisen so high that in their return they were several times almost drowned.

It was an easy thing for Esau to sell his "brithright," but it was not so easy to get it back. Poor man he sought a place for repentance and could nowhere find it.

Thus the pilgrims became lost in the darkness, and weary and alarmed at the storm, they found shelter near by, and there they sat down to await the break of day. But being weary they fell asleep. Just as soon as the christian becomes weary of the journey, and sits down to wait for the day of sunshine, he will be very apt to fall asleep spiritually, and like the Pilgrim of old, will awake to scenes most unpleasant. Not far from where the pilgrims slept, was a castle called,

"*Doubting Castle,*"

the owner whereof was "Giant Despair." Every morning this great giant would rise up early and walk over his grounds to see if, perchance, some pilgrim had wandered upon his grounds, and if he found any such he would take them prisoners. In his rounds that morning he came across Christian and Hopeful. Going up to them he called them to awake. At this they were startled, for upon opening their eyes they beheld standing before them one that terrified them. Alas, their eyes were opened when too late.

Many are thus sleeping, feeling perfectly secure, but sooner or later their eyes will be opened to that which will be most alarming. Sickness, or some sudden calamity, will befall them and then will follow the regret. Suddenly summoned to the bar of God in their sinful condition, how will such stand the judgment of God! What will they do at the swelling of the Jordan?

Christian and Hopeful were quickly driven on before the Giant into "Doubting Castle." There they were lodged in a very dark dungeon. After being left there for some time without anything to eat or drink, they received a visit from the Giant, who came upon them with a club and most sorely beat the pilgrims until they were not able to help themselves. Then, he left them in all their misery for a day or two, when he visited them a second time, advising them to kill themselves, and thus be saved from all this torture. After he left, the prisoners began to talk over their troubles, and at last Christian, discouraged and despondent, turned to Hopeful saying, "What shall we do? The life we now live is miserable. For my part I know not whether it is best to live thus, or to die."

Then he added, "My soul chooseth strangling rather than life, and the grave is more easy for me than this dungeon."

We are reminded of poor old Job, when during a fit of despondency he said of life, "I loathe it; I would not live always: let me alone, for my days are vanity." But worse still was the advice Job's wife gave him when she said to him, "Curse God and die." In other words, "Commit suicide." Thus, there are times in life when the discouraged ask the same question. "Why do I live? Does it pay to live? Would I not be better off by blowing out the candle?"

Such promptings are the whispers of the devil in the ear of the disheartened. But to yield to such whispers, is not only sinful in the extreme, but the act of a coward.

In all cases of suicide on the part of the head of the family, none is meaner than to destroy self for fear of coming to want. Let such rather boldly breast the slings and arrows of adverse fortune, and present the strong arm and a devoted heart to wife and children. Such suicides are purely selfish, and there is not one single redeeming feature, but rather a bold confession of cowardice and baseness, to say nothing of the sin against God. It is well written,

"When all the blandishments of life are gone,
The coward sneaks to death: the brave live on."

Instead of asking, "Is life worth living?" it were better to ask calmly, "Is death worth dying?" and in reply to that question there is a ready answer, "No, it is not worth dying until one has finished his life's work, and has well earned the grave in which his body is to lie, when once the life has departed in its natural way. Then, and only then, is death worth dying.

No wonder Hopeful rebuked Christian for his temporary and momentary seeming insanity, by reminding him of the great sin of which he spoke. "My brother," said Hopeful, "thou talkest of ease in the grave; but hast thou forgotten the hell whither for certain all such deliberate self destroying persons go?"

The better and wiser course for such despondent persons to pursue is for them to consider the future and its possibilities, rather than the sad past with its discouragements. Besides, a glimpse at the past would remind many such of their triumphs amid their trials. Christian seems to have forgotten the triumphs of the past. At one time he was attacked by Apollyon, when death seemed inevitable; but he was conqueror, and triumphed over his discouragements. He also forgot the lions, which he thought would tear him to pieces, but when once he came up to them he found them chained. He seems also to have forgotten all about the "Valley of the Shadow of Death," when at every moment death appeared sure. And yet, with all these trials, he still lived, for he had triumphed over all. Why not, therefore, try to triumph rather than suffer defeat like a coward?

There are times when things don't go just as we might wish them, but instead of surrendering, and thereby showing our weakness, let us rather be like brave soldiers. Don't be a coward, but "quit you like men."

Then, too, it might be well for many to consider a little more carefully just what often leads to such fits of despondency.

It is not real active service, but rather when one gets out of the right way. Christian never before had any such thoughts of self destruction. His dispondency arose, only after he had stepped aside from the way of the Lord.

The devil is the one to prompt self destruction. Had Elijah stood boldly up for the God he had so forcibly revealed at the time when he called down fire from heaven, he would not have been asking God that he might die. But, fleeing from the presence of God and duty, and hiding away in idleness in the mountains of Horeb, he there preferred death to life. Get out of your cave, out into the sunshine of God's vineyard of active service and duty, and you will not have time to be thinking about dying, but will rather think how you can best live and serve. Look about you and see the many demands which appeal to you, in the home, in the church, and as a citizen. You owe much to others. See to it then that you fulfil all your obligations before you talk about dying.

Christian and Hopeful, however, were given a further trial in Doubting Castle, for the Giant paid them a third visit and finding them still alive, he took them out into a yard and there showed them the bones of men who had been slain, and told them that in a week's time he would tear them in pieces as he had done to others before them. After he departed, the pilgrims thought much about what they had seen and heard until at last they lay down to sleep. At midnight they began to pray, and continued in prayer until almost daybreak. "What a fool I have been," said Christian, "to lie in this dungeon, when I may as well walk at liberty!"

Hopeful looked at him in astonishment wondering what he meant.

"I have

a key in my bosom called Promise,

that will, I am persuaded, open any lock in Doubting Castle."

What a revelation and what good news! At once they took the key and began to try at the dungeon door, and to their happy surprise, the bolt turned and the door opened. Thus, at each door they used the key and with but little difficulty each door was opened, until they found themselves at the outer gate. Here it was a little more difficult, but at last the bolt moved, and the gate opened.

Many others are locked up in "Castles of Doubt" and despondency, out of which they might go if only they would use the proper means. A few more prayers to Him from whence "cometh our help" would result in opening many closed castles and prisons of soul torture. Many are to-day in dungeons of despair who could find much relief, if they would not be too proud to ask God for help. Some only laugh at the thought of prayer, but experience has taught many its blessings.

Too frequently prayer is the last resort. People will try all manner of experiments and spend much time in endeavoring to escape from their troubles, until, amid discouragements, some would rather die than live. One stroke comes after the other, and one visitation of trouble follows the other, like the visits of the Giant to Christian. Each day a Giant Despair adds new blows, till death itself seems to stare them in the face. Prayer, however, has caused many such to say as did Christian, "What a fool I have been to lie in a dungeon, when I may as well walk at liberty." The great trouble with many is they have locked themselves up in the room of their little self until the door of Doubt has become sealed, and there appears to be no way of escape. Their eyes are blinded to all the precious Promises of God. Promises! why yes, take down God's word as it lies neglected and dust covered, take it down from its resting place. Blow off the dust and look within for its rich Promises. God's promises know of no such thing as "Despair." "God is love," and His promises are rounds in the ladder up which we climb to heaven. Are you down at the foot of the ladder? Then begin climbing by taking hold of God's Promises. Hold fast the faith. Take strong hold and press toward the mark. You will never get to heaven by sitting down in the Castle of Despair. Resting in such places is to rest upon another's grounds, who will sooner or later take you prisoner, and in his dungeon you will have to suffer the penalty of his sentence. "The way of the transgressor is hard," and such as will walk in that way need not complain if they are beaten with many stripes, and robbed of all their possessions.

The misfortune with some is they allow themselves to be led on by those who are known as "Vain Confidence." These men and women are so sure of their own safety in the way of the world that they even laugh at such as would do good. Let them see a man endeavor to do that which is right, and they ridicule his faith in the Lord. If he is seen to go to the house of God for worship, he is laughed at for his piety. If he spends his evenings at home with his wife and children, he is held up as one who is "tied to his wife's apron string." There are many just such characters of "Vain-Confidence," who deride in others whatever is noble and good.

Many a happy home has thus been destroyed, and many a once true follower of God has been led away from Him by this very class of people. If there are any such men or women among your associates, you had better abandon their company at once, for they will sooner or later prove your ruin. They will lead you on until at last they suddenly disappear. You look for them and they are gone. You call but receive no answer. They have either fallen into the pit themselves, or having led you into it, they forsake you. You want a friend, some assistance, but they are conspicuously absent. Remember, you are in a sense, your own best friend, and far better please yourself by doing that which is right, than "follow a multitude to do evil," for when once you are in trouble, your old friends who led you into pits of misfortune and castles of despair, will not help you. Such persons you will do well to call, not friends, but only acquaintances, and the less you know of them by way of association, the better it will be for you in the end.

It may all be pleasing at first, but it is well to profit by the sad ending of such as have not been wise.

No wonder that Christian when he had safely escaped from the miserable Castle was moved to warn others. His experience had proven so very bitter that he was unwilling for any others to share his sad fate. He, therefore, erected a pillar and upon the side of it had engraven, "Over this stile is the way to Doubting Castle, which is kept by Giant Despair, who despiseth the King of the Celestial City, and seeks to destroy his holy pilgrims."

God has thus had planted many sign boards along the way of life, to warn men. His holy word is filled with sentences which tell travelers of dangerous places. The way of the drunkard, the glutton, the licentious, the transgressor, the lukewarm, the backslider, and a hundred other dangerous paths, are all clearly pointed out in God's holy Word, and the traveler to the Celestial City will do well to study diligently his Guide Book and guard against the "easy paths," for they but lead to despair.

Reader, how are you conducting yourself? Are you a professed follower of God? Then do not complain because you have a few trials in life. Don't look for some "easy way." Don't complain because you have too much to do for the Lord. Few Christians have ever suffered from doing too much for God and the church. Many, however, have suffered from doing too little. If you are in Doubting

Castle, on the grounds of the enemy, then get out of it at once, for should death overtake you in that Castle, where would you belong? The Lord would not be likely to look for any of His people in that abode. Falling at such places, the devil would but naturally come to claim his own. Take heed, therefore, to your steps, and looking unto Jesus as your Leader, hear Him say unto you, "follow me."

CHAPTER IX.
ATHEISM—SCEPTICISM—INFIDELITY.

IN his journey, Christian met with a man who was an Atheist. Atheist, like many others of his tribe, was no doubt miserable, and was anxious to meet with some one who thought as he did. Misery loves company and goes forth in search of like conditions. Thus it is with many who are bold in infidelity and unbelief. They are not at ease; their conscience is ill at rest. Something within them seems to disturb their quiet repose, and they roam about in search of some one who may happen to believe as they claim to in their false belief. Accordingly, they are ever ready to start an argument in hope of winning some one on their side for company's sake.

It was so with the man who met with Christian. At once he inquired of Christian whither he was going, and when he answered, "we are going to mount Zion," then

"Atheist fell into a very great laughter."

This seems to be the almost general practice of his followers ever since. Laughter and derision, form in a large measure the points of argument with many of the infidels and unbelievers of to-day. They point to the time of Creation and because some things are not in accordance with their own limited understanding, they laugh at the works, and ridicule the idea of Christian belief in God's works of creation. The Flood in the eyes of the infidel is a thing of ridicule, and they but laugh at those who believe in the Sacred account of the Deluge. The history of the parting of the waters of the Red Sea by the Divine command of God is laughed at by such men. They would either destroy the whole account, or else explain it by mere chance of a sudden change of winds whereby the waters parted.

And so all through the Word of God, they would explain away all miraculous accounts by their argument of "laughter and ridicule." When Christian asked in surprise why Atheist laughed, the answer he received was, "I laugh to see what ignorant persons you are to take upon you so tedious a journey, and yet are likely to have nothing but your travel for your pains."

At first thought it might seem that such men are harmless, and their "laughter" but empty dreams, but upon a more careful consideration of the results of such men's impious profession, we behold a very grave subject, demanding the most serious consideration.

There are a number of reasons why Infidelity and Scepticism are dangerous and most undesirable. First of all, they tend to destroy the real truth.

Such men would trample under foot the very Truth itself, God's Word. They would make of it merely a book printed and sold for the money that is in it, like any other book. So far as the Inspiration of the Bible is concerned, they only laugh at such an idea. And yet, were they to attempt to write anything like the Bible, they would either be converted to God in such an effort, or else would be thoroughly disgusted at their utter failure to reproduce anything like the inspired Word of God. It is that very fact that makes the Bible a book unique. No one is able to write a book like it, because it is God's Word, and God's thoughts are not man's thoughts, nor is God's book man's work. The Story of Ruth as it is written in the Bible is a story that no man is capable of reproducing. Any effort to write a story like it would be as fruitless as an effort to reproduce upon canvas a sunset.

Our very best artists are able to produce something like the sunset in a faint picture, but nothing at all equal to the sunset itself. And so it is with an effort to write either the whole of the Bible or a single part of it. The end of such an effort would be only a preposterous undertaking.

Besides, what better than the Bible does the unbeliever and infidel offer? They would destroy the real Truth, without giving anything else instead, in any manner whatever, to compensate for that which they take away. Even were the Truth of the word of God but weak and imperfect, yet, it would be better than nothing, and nothing is what the infidel gives. A stick or cane may be imperfect in its execution, and yet, it is a support for the aged and infirm, and helps them on in their journey. It would be a mean man who would dare to knock out from under an old man the cane on which he had been leaning, and let him fall helpless by the roadside. Is it not equally base in any man who comes along trying to destroy the Truth, knocking thus from under the aged the very support which has been their help all along the way of life? Many men and women have gone leaning upon God's Word down to the grave, and the Bible has been unto them a support. Others are leaning upon this same support, and for any man to come along and endeavor to knock out from under them that very staff is to say the least, base, and the work of a mean person. If a man prefers to drag along helplessly to the grave and death without any hope, then let him go alone, and not endeavor to drag down others with him to hell. If such men prefer to sail across the great sea of life in darkness, to land at last at the haven of Despair, then let them be content to be wrecked alone, without trying to destroy the Lighthouse which lights others, enabling them safely to reach the haven of rest. If they find pleasure in groping for their way in the darkness of Chance, then let them not be vile enough to tear to pieces the Chart which others have studied, and which has given them their moorings, and enabled them to find the true way, Christ Jesus. If the infidel and sceptic prefer, in their own strength, to steer their boat across the great deep, then let them do so without endeavoring to plan for the removal of Christ from such as have taken Him as their Great Pilot. If they are willing to be shipwrecked of all hope, let them not be so base as to attempt the destruction of the life-boats of others.

Such men, legally, would be subject to the laws of the land, and if because in spiritual things they are allowed for a time to escape the just condemnation for their offences, they should at least from a sense of common courtesy and propriety, not try to harm others, even though for the time they may happen to escape punishment. Until they have something better to offer, it were better, yes, more honorable, for such men to keep quiet, and not thrust their offences in the faces of others who are perfectly happy and satisfied with "the good old way and the good old paths."

What must we think of a man who would take away the bread from the very mouth of the hungry, without giving something better instead? You would feel disposed to call such a man a thief and villain. But what would you call a man who sneeringly snatches the very Bread of Life from such as hunger and thirst after righteousness, giving instead only ashes?

Infidelity, in short, is nothing more nor less than a hurricane. Its chief mission seems to be that of destruction. It tears down, without attempting to build up. Unable to create, it contents itself in destroying.

There is another argument against infidelity in that it tends to increase crime by attempting to overthrow the doctrine of future rewards and punishment. Even if there were no future beyond the grave, yet, the very thought of future rewards and punishment tends to check crime, and increase virtue. Take away all thought of a future beyond that of this present life, and there will be many more to turn their thoughts toward iniquity and crime. Society, instead of being elevated, would become more and more polluted and corrupt. It is the fear of future punishment that puts a check upon crime, and keeps many transgressors from doing things of which they would otherwise be guilty. Conscience is a great power for checking evil doers, but fear coupled to that power gives a wonderful impetus for the bridling of evil passions.

Take away all thought of God in the world, and all fear of future punishment for the wicked, and you open the very flood gates into society, through which will come pouring a torrent of vice and crime. Society would soon become so honey-combed with evil that in a short time the very heart of it would be consumed by the disease of iniquity to the forfeiting of its very best things, and the wrecking of many lives. From a prisoner in Pentonville prison, London, came this letter. "I am one of thirteen infidels. Where are my friends? Four have been hanged. One became a Christian. Six have been sentenced to various terms of imprisonment, and one is now confined in a cell just over my head, sentenced to imprisonment for life."

These few words very forcibly tell of the pernicious effects of infidel teachings and sentiments. Out of thirteen infidels twelve suffered for breaking the laws of their country. One escaped from breaking the civil laws but how? In what manner did he differ from the other twelve? He became a Christian. Not that all infidels are transgressors of the law. No one would for a moment so argue, but infidel teachings tend to make transgressors of the law, and spread crime, for reasons already stated. The general tendency of infidelity and scepticism is evil. If you sow to the wind you can only reasonably expect to reap the whirlwind. Gather together all the criminals of the land, and see the large percentage of that number that are sceptical in their belief. The letter from the infidel prisoner would doubtless explain the secret history of many other criminals.

Few men have ever had their morals elevated by infidelity. But very many have had their morals most decidedly lowered through its teachings.

One of the great teachers of this pernicious doctrine ridiculed the idea of "an infinite God making failures, in that some of His creatures are eternally lost." He argued that if there be a God, he has made a mistake in the works of his creation in thus creating an imperfect being. But it is not God's fault that some are lost. This same person, who criticised God for his mistakes, says, "If I have a soul, I've got to save it."

Although God helps a man, and in a sense God saves the soul, (for salvation is of the Lord,) yet, in another sense, man must help to save that soul, for if man so desires, he can destroy his soul. From the infidel's own argument, therefore, man can save his soul or he can destroy it, and it is no fault of God that some prefer to lose their soul. As, therefore, the infidel writer says, "If I have a soul I've got to save it," he should have completed the thought along his own line of argument and added, "If I have a soul and lose it, it is my own fault."

The doctrine of future punishment, therefore, is no indication of a failure on the part of God to create a perfect being, but only a result of man's own failure to keep pure and good as God made him. The bridge may be perfectly secure and carry safely across large

multitudes. But the safety and even perfection of the bridge does not prevent a man from leaping over the side of the structure and hurling himself into the deep waters beneath. So God has made man a free and independent creature, to do good or evil. God has given man freedom above the beasts of the fields or the fowls of the air, and God has further given man the advice to do good, and has warned him against evil, but man is left to make his own choice. Had God made man that he could not have sinned, then God would have robbed man of his independence and freedom. Man would then have been only a piece of machinery, a mere tool.

Another argument against infidelity is that it undermines a nation's safety. Infidel France, which is pointed to by one of our infidel writers as an illustration of the progress of a nation that is infidel in its teachings, is a very good illustration of the fact that infidelity undermines a nation's safety.

Look back into the history of France at a time when infidelity was greatest, what was its evil influence? The fourth of October, 1789, when such men gathered together at Clubs and plotted the Bread War by forbidding the bakers to bake bread, was but the beginning of the fruits of infidelity to that country. The next morning Paris was alive with powers threatening the overthrow of that nation. When, therefore, an infidel writer says, "I find just in proportion as people have been religious, in proportion they have gone back to barbarism," his statement is not true. The opposite, however, is a fact, namely, in proportion as a nation is irreligious, that nation borders on to barbarism. The "Reign of Terrors" in France is a sad blot for infidelity and its dangerous teachings. Let Atheism and Infidelity rule this land of ours for a few years, and we, too, would return to barbarism, and would be ushered into a terrible "Reign of Terrors" that would soak our land with human blood. What has infidelity ever done for the betterment of society, or the elevation of morals? What has it done for the care of suffering humanity, by way of looking after the poor, the sick or the aged?

And when such persons come down to the hour of death, what is their comfort or consolation? What hope have they? Alas! they are without both God and hope, and are left to die in misery and remorse. When Col. Ethan Allen, a notorious infidel, was asked by his sick and dying daughter, "Father I am about to die: shall I believe the principles which you have taught me, or shall I believe what mother taught me," the infidel after waiting a few moments to calm his remorse for his evil teachings, answered, saying, "Believe what your mother has taught you."

There are many others who would not want their children to die in the belief of their own teachings.

Such a father once went to Annapolis for his son who had just returned from Libby prison. He found his son dying, and was asked by the chaplain to inform him of his nearness to death. But the father refused, saying to the chaplain, "You tell him, and especially tell him to prepare for the future. I have been an unbeliever, a wicked man; but my son's mother is a Christian, and he had better follow her."

What then is there in infidelity that is worth possession? In life it is deadly poison and dangerous in its influence. In death it is only wretched remorse to the soul.

We are not surprised, therefore, at Voltaire, who, one day when he had dining with him two other infidels, stopped them at once from conversing about atheism, saying to them, "Wait till my servants have withdrawn: I do not wish to have my throat cut to-night."

Some of these men remind one of the man who manufactured a certain kind of patent medicine which he claimed very good for a certain kind of sickness among children. His own child took sick of that very disease, and when asked why he did not give his child some of the medicine he had manufactured for that disorder, he replied, saying, "I make that medicine to sell, and not to use." So it is with much of the teaching of infidels and sceptics. They are ready to broadcast it, but very few would be willing to feed their own children upon that kind of poisonous doctrine.

Upon all infidel barges might well be written the inscription, "Without God and without hope;" and woe is that parent who would place his own child upon such a deadly barge to be carried on to the rapids of darkness and despair. Scepticism and infidelity are but confusing and deadly. Hume, the historian once said, "I seem affrighted and confounded with the solitude in which I am placed by my philosophy. When I look abroad, on every side I see dispute, contradiction, and distraction. When I turn my eye inward, I find nothing but doubt and ignorance. Where am I? From what cause do I derive my existence? To what condition shall I return? I am confounded with questions. I begin to fancy myself in a very deplorable condition, environed with darkness on every side."

Hume's philosophy of scepticism and infidelity did not give him very much light, but, extinguishing from him every star of hope, and severing the ties which bound him to his Creator, his miserable philosophy left him to swing out upon an ocean of darkness, uncertainty and despair.

At the funeral of one such more recently, strong men declared that nothing had ever appealed to them so strongly before for religion and Christianity as the utter desolation and hopelessness of the family of mourners. Not a word of consolation, not a soothing note of music, not a prayer for sympathy or help or mercy.

Thus, with no hope for future union, no consolation in Christian faith, no solace in religion, the utter loneliness and dreariness which enveloped the bereaved, was something which words cannot express.

In view of all this, it is not only wise, but sensible to say the least, to abandon all talk of scepticism and infidelity, and to take hold of that which gives hope and salvation. The religion of Christ is good for little children, causing them to grow up an honor to their parents. That religion is also good for our youth, making of them noble citizens, and a blessing to morals and society. The religion of Christ, is good for old age, and enables such as have lived through life, to review the past with the sweet satisfaction of knowing they have not lived in vain, and of the comfortable assurance of everlasting bliss with the redeemed at last in glory above. Better even "hate" the world, home and friends who are so minded, than follow their teachings, and "hate" God. Let God be true, and others liars.

CHAPTER X.
OVER THE RIVER INTO THE CELESTIAL CITY.

THE present life is often not very encouraging to the Christian. It frequently so happens that the wicked prosper, while the christian has his trials and discouragements. But "there remaineth a rest for the people of God." Dives may have his good things in this present life, while Lazarus has his misfortunes, but there comes a day when God properly adjusts all things, each one receiving his reward according to his own just deserts. Paul had a hard time of it all along the line of his christian experience, but he "pressed toward the mark." "Onward" is the call to the followers of God, with the injunction "not to grow weary in well doing."

So it was with Christian. Had he confined his vision simply to the present, and lost all sight of the future, then he might well have become discouraged in his journey, for from the very outstart he had nothing but discouragements. He had no sooner gotten up on the mount than he was compelled to descend again into the valley. But the journey has an end. Life is not a continuous circle. It not only has a beginning, but an end, and the end of the righteous is "rest" and "peace." Says Bunyan, "I saw in my dream that by this time the pilgrims were over the Enchanted ground, and were entering into

the Country of Beulah.

Here the air was very sweet and pleasant. Not only no sickness there but a place of singing. Being beyond the valley of death, it was also a place of perfect safety. Surely, it must be near the end of the journey. So it was, for from that place they obtained a glimpse of the City of God. There they might well sing:

> "O Beulah land, sweet Beulah land,
> As on thy highest mount I stand,
> I look away across the sea,
> Where mansions are prepared for me,
> And view the shining glory shore,
> My heaven, my home forevermore."

Here also the contract between the Bride and the Bridegroom was renewed. There they heard voices from heaven saying: "Say ye to the daughter of Zion; behold, his reward is with him."

So the christian will at last enter the land of Beulah, for the prophet says: "Thou shalt no more be termed Forsaken; neither shall thy land any more be termed Desolate, but shall be called the land of Beulah," for the Lord delighteth in thee, and thy land shall be married." "As a young man marrieth a virgin, so shall thy sons marry thee; and as the bridegroom rejoiceth over the bride, so shall thy God rejoice over thee."

Traveling in such a Beulah land, the christian may well sing:

"The zephyrs seem to float to me,
Sweet sounds of heaven's melody."

And, as the redeemed of the Lord continue their journey amid such rapturous scenes, they exclaim,

"The Saviour comes, and walks with me,
And sweet communion here have we;
He gently leads me by His hand,
For this is heaven's border-land."

As the aged Christian lifted up his eyes, lo Heaven was now very near. His step may have been feeble, while his trembling hand held firmly to the cane. His cheek doubtless hollow with age and trials, while his eyes were sunken and dim.

Between the Pilgrims and the City of God, lay the Jordon. At first, they were timid to enter, but as they by faith stepped into the river of death, the waters parted, and they passed over safely. The less fearful the dying christian is, the more shallow are the waters of the Jordon of death. But after all, the river of death is a blessing, for it is the "dressing room" of heaven. The soul enters the river on this side in corruption, and is raised on the other side in incorruption. It enters on this side in weakness, and is raised on the other side in strength. It enters on this side a natural body, and is raised on the

other side a spiritual body. That river of death washes away all the infirmities of the believer in Christ. No need of a cane on the other side, for the christian comes forth redeemed, washed in the "blood of the Lamb." As we look upon the old structure of the body on this side of the river, we see "the silver cord loosed, the golden bowl broken, the pitcher broken at the fountain, the wheel broken at the cistern." But looking again on the other side of the river of death, we behold "the dust returning to the earth as it was, while the spirit returns to God who gave it." "For we know that if our earthly house of this tabernacle were dissolved, we have a building of God, a house not made with hands, eternal in the heavens"

Scarcely had Christian come forth from the Jordon, than he was met by angels who had come to welcome him into the Celestial City. They began to tell of the glory of Zion, the tree of life, and of the beauty of the place in general. "No sickness; no sorrow; no tears; no death." "Former things passed away." "Reap what you have sown." Oh, what tidings of joy greeted the pilgrim just beyond the river! Some christians have hard times here, but a happy surprise awaits them just beyond the river.

At last the pilgrims reached the gate of the Celestial City. Over it was written in letters of gold, "Blessed are they that do his commandments, that they may have right to the tree of life. and may enter in through the gates into the city."

Standing thus

before the Golden Gate,

the pilgrims sent in their certificate, which they had received at the "Wicket Gate."

Then the King commanded to open the gate, "that the righteous may enter in."

But as they entered a most wonderful change took place. Their raiment shone like gold. On their heads were crowns, while harps were placed in their hands. Heaven itself seemed to rejoice at the entrance of souls into that heavenly city, for the bells in the city rang, and there was rejoicing everywhere. Added to all this there was a grand chorus from the redeemed: "Enter ye into the joy of thy Lord," and the gates were closed.

Beholding the grand spectacle he did, it was not much wonder that Bunyan wrote saying, "I wished myself among them."

With such a prize before the christian, he may well press forward through all manner of perils and misfortunes, for at the end of his journey he will be more than repaid for all the sacrifices made, and the sufferings endured for the cause of Christ. Even with this most glorious account, as given by Bunyan, of the end of the redeemed in glory, yet "Not half has been told."

Would that this beautiful story might end thus, and like it, all lives. But, as Bunyan stood gazing, he looked around, and behold, "Ignorance" came up to the river, and crossed over. He went alone to the gate. No angels came forward to greet him. As he read the inscription over the gateway, he began to knock. An angel appeared and asked him for his certificate. In his confusion and embarassment he began to feel in his bosom, but found none.

The two shining ones who met Christian and Hopeful now appeared; not to accompany "Ignorance" into the City, as they had Christian and Hopeful, but they "bound him hand and foot." Then flying off through the air, they carried him by the gate of heaven to "the door in the side of a hill, and put him there." And Bunyan adds, "Then I saw that there was a way to hell even from the gate of heaven, as well as from the City of Destruction." "Ignorance" had laughed at Christian and Hopeful in their endeavors, but now in the end he discovered when, alas, too late, that they were right and he wrong.

Look then, if you will at the end of the righteous. Like the pilgrims they finally reach the Celestial City, and enter through the gates into glory.

When "Ignorance" was asked on what ground he expected to enter the celestial gate he answered, "On the ground of morality, of being a good liver, and an honest man." But the true follower of God pleads only the merits of Jesus Christ for his entrance into that blessed city, for "there is no other name given among men, whereby we can be saved."

However, with the pardon of sins by faith in the Lord Jesus Christ, then at the gate of heaven the christian hears the plaudit,

"Well done." "Come ye blessed of my father." Then with palms of victory and crowns of glory, they sing, "Holy, holy, holy is the Lord."

New joys are ever being added. We look upon the faces once marked with care, but now all the lines are removed. Faces that were once pale and sickly, are now a picture of the bloom of youth. Bodies that were once afflicted, are now without "spot of blemish." There, amid unspeakable joys, they sing, not the songs of earth, but the Song of Moses and the Lamb, saying, "Blessing, and honor, and glory, and power, be unto Him that sitteth upon the throne, and unto the Lamb, for ever and ever."

> "Oh ! then what raptured greetings
> On heaven's happy shore ;
> What knitting severed friendships up,
> Where partings are no more !"

The mere description of a place, affords a vague conception of what the reality is. Neither artist nor poet can do justice to a sunset, a rainbow or a waterfall. It is like trying to describe to a blind man the beauties of a landscape, or the glories of the Grand Canyon of the Yellowstone. So in regard to Heaven. "Eye hath not seen," and no one has returned to tell us of that at which we are now beholding "through a glass darkly." Indeed, we are tempted to exclaim as did the poet, "Strange, is it not, that, of the myriads who before us passed the door of darkness through, not one, returns to tell us of the road, which, to discover, we must travel too.

The Bible, however, happily, throws some light upon the Distant City. As the Astronomer with the telescope brings the far distant Artic Planets Uranus and Neptune within the vision of mortal eye, so the telescope of the Word of God, brings Heaven within the vision of man; for in turning on the Light of Divine Revelation, we catch bright rays of the Heavenly City of God. As such, it tells us that Heaven is a Place. Heaven, is a term used to express the positive issue or consummation of the dispensation of redemption, or the end of such as will be saved. As regards the location of Heaven we are largely left to conjecture, and yet, our general impressions lead us to believe it is somewhere above us. Christ in

His ascension rose up from Mount Oliver. "Elijah went up by a whirlwind into heaven.

This earth of ours does not afford very many places suitable for Heaven. No such place as yet has ever been discovered on earth. There is too much suffering and sickness and sin on earth for it to ever be a suitable place. It is true that this earth could by the power of God be changed into "a new heaven and earth," but meantime where is heaven? Surely, the dead are not all sleeping in the grave awaiting the general resurrection, for "to be absent from the body is to be present with the Lord," and Paul once wrote saying "to depart and be with Christ is far better," and surely he would never have so written, if he had thought death meant lying in the grave until the last trumpet call. "This day shalt thou be with me in paradise," said Christ to the repenting thief upon the cross.

Earth is nothing more than the "footstool" of God, while heaven is His throne. When Christ was about to leave the apostles, He said to them, "I go to prepare a place for you," and that place is not on earth, but in Heaven as it now is, heaven was then already existing, but Christ meant to say that He would go and there prepare for them a place in that heaven. He also speaks of "coming" again to "receive" them unto himself, that "where he is there they may be also." And the apostle reminds us of the fact, that "if our earthly house of this tabernacle be dissolved, we have an house not made with hands, eternal in the heavens." As the redeemed are limited, finite beings, with glorified bodies, they must exist somewhere; they must have a definite location; that somewhere for the redeemed, is called heaven.

There are also conditions of the redeemed. Not a general medley of persons gathered together without order, for one of the first laws of heaven is order. When Christ fed the five thousand, there was order. He had them seated in companies of fifties and hundreds, otherwise there would have been utter confusion. So in heaven, there will be order and no confusion. As to who is to "have the first seat in glory," that kind of selfishness and jealousy, is confined wholly to this present life. The present life, however, will largely determine the condition of the future in heaven. Each one on earth is fashioned for a heavenly place. Every christian is designed for a special place in glory. In the building of the first and most beautiful of all Temples for worship, the stones were all carefully prepared in the quarry, so that when the temple was erected, they all fit together so perfectly, that there was neither ax nor hammer, nor any tool of iron heard in the temple while it was being erected. So, God would have it in heaven.

This Divine Order naturally involves variety among the redeemed. It is very true that all in heaven will be satisfied, and perfectly happy, so much so that each will say "my cup runneth over," but some cups will be larger than others, and the capacities will differ somewhat along the lines as they exist among christians in this life, for "one star differeth from another star in glory."

Accordingly, is not this only natural and as it should be? It would appear but just that the men and women who, other things being equal, having given their consecration to God and the church, should have larger capacities for the glories of heaven than those who having had the same opportunities, failed to "redeem the time," but waited until death frightened them, and then surrendered themselves to do the will of the Father.

Among heaven's most illustrous, therefore, will be those whose hearts are fixed upon holy things. It will not be a matter of Creeds or particular church, but "the pure in heart shall see God," where there shall be "one Lord, one faith, one Baptism, one God and Father of us all." Paul with his life of consecration to God, will surely have larger capacities for the riches of heaven, than the thief who on the cross, confessed Christ. The are "pillars" in the temple of God, and they are those who were the "pillars" here on earth; the St. Catherines, the Dorcasses, the Johns, the consecrated men and women in the church of God. These, will be among the illustrious in heaven. Many who are now little noticed will be among the bright stars, for they are meekly but devoutly doing God's will here on earth, in going about doing good.

Unhappily, there are many professed christians who are living a "zig-zag" life. At one time near Christ, then following afar off. Such persons cannot reasonably expect to be among the brighter stars in glory.

Another class of persons that will appear among the brighter stars in glory, will be, the sore afflicted in Christ.

If during the process of building, the corner stones could speak, they would doubtless do considerable murmuring, and would ask, "Why are we so hammered?" But when the building is completed, then there is visible evidence for the hammering and carving. It was to make more useful and beautiful the stones; and so we are to be the spiritual stones for the temple of God in glory, and there is need of removing some of the rough corners, the superfluities of life, in order that we may be all the more beautiful for that house not made with hands, eternal in the heavens.

The Apostle once caught a glimpse of some who were nearest the throne in heaven, and in his ecstasy, he asked, "Who are these in white array before the throne?" And the Angel answered, "These are they which came up out of great tribulation, therefore, are they before the throne." Such, are among the "pillars" in heaven, for it takes the soil of affliction to grow the tall cedars of Lebanon for the temple of God. "If we suffer with him, we shall also reign with him."

Are any in distress? The apostle encourages such by saying, "Be not weary in well doing, for in due season we shall reap if we faint not." And Paul adds at another time, "I reckon, that the sufferings of the present are not worthy to be compared to the glories that shall be revealed in us," "for, our light afflictions work for us a far more exceeding and eternal weight of glory." In sickness, sorrow, afflictions and adversity, God is preparing material for the "pillars" and corner stones, for his temple in glory.

Will we know each other in heaven? Natural reasoning would surely teach us to say, "Yes," and inspiration teaches the same. Otherwise, there could not well be that large degree of happiness.

The power of friendship is universally known here on earth. One is not apt to be so happy among strangers as among acquaintances and friends, and if in heaven there were no recognition, then there would be wanting one of the chief requisites for happiness. Recognition begets joy. Let old acquaintances, who may have been separated for a long time, meet, and how joyful the greetings. They may not at first recognize each other, but in the course of conversation, or in the singing of a song, the chamber of memory is unlocked, and old friends once more are in each others fond embrace. This will be one of the great joys of heaven; the meeting of friends, the recalling of fond memories, and the reuniting of friendships, which had been partly broken by death.

But, some one may ask, "Will not recognition mar happiness, in that some dear friend may be absent?" We answer, "No," for conditions will be changed, and there will be realized fully the justice of God, and all will be willing to conform to God's judgments and works. Heavenly recognition, is also reasonable, because memory will continue, and the social nature will remain. Destroy memory and you destroy individuality, and heaven would not be heaven. Memory will ever enrich the treasures of joy of the redeemed soul.

But again, some one may ask, "Will not memory mar happiness in the recalling of early sins." In answer to this question, we again answer, "No," for Christ has very clearly and definitely declared that He "will blot out all sin," so that there "shall be no more remembrance forever" of the pardoned sin. When Christ forgives sins, He blots it out of his memory and never more refers to it.

Nor will the existence of the social nature in heaven mar the happiness. It is frequently asked, "What of those who have been married two or three times? Suppose in heaven the different husbands or different wives meet, will not there be some jealousy, and the pleasures of heaven affected because of the existence of the social nature in the recognition?" This question has also been very forcibly answered in God's holy word, that in heaven "they neither marry nor are given in marriage." So enlarged will be our views, that there will be no "evil eye," for "nothing entereth heaven that defileth." On the other hand, the social nature will greatly add to the joys of the heavenly state and life. There will be such reunions as Caleb and Joshua, David and Jonathan, the members of the Bethany home, the reunion of families and congregations, all of which will make heaven the ideal place.

Recognition is further evident from the numerous Scriptural references. When David lost his little boy in death, he had no question as to his future meeting with and recognition of his child. "He shall not return to me, but I shall go to him," was the conscious knowledge that gave to a bereaved father comfort and consolation in the hour of sorrow. That same consciousness and hope, has comforted many parents since.

Notwithstanding the fact that Moses had died fifteen hundred years before, and Elias nearly one thousand years, yet they were recognized on the Mount of Transfiguration.

Paul also believed in heavenly recognition, for he speaks of the special love for his own converts, and his hope of their heavenly reunion. It was doubtless in view of this that Paul wrote saying, "Then shall I know as I also am known." Although faith may be lost in sight and hope in fruition, yet "love never faileth," nor will it fail in heaven.

Christ gave back to the widow of Nain, not "*a*" son, but "*her*" son. He promised to the bereaved sisters, not "Lazarus," but "your *brother* shall rise." And there is a promise left to the righteous that they shall "sit down with Abraham and Isaac and Jacob in the kingdom of heaven," implying most clearly that these men shall be recognized in heaven, and if they, then others, "for we shall know as we are known."

The fact of heavenly recognition will afford an opportunity of expressing unexpressed gratitude. Here on earth the opportunity is often not afforded. At the time results are not seen, while frequently death cuts down its victim before an opportunity is given for expressions of love and gratitude. Accordingly, many pass from earth to glory in clouds of disappointments. Parents thus often pass away with disappointments as regards their children, while christian men and women often see so few visible fruits of their labors that they are inclined to think their lives have been a failure.

heaven, however, will unfold some of the sweet memories of the past. In heaven there will be many happy surprises. The results of good works will there be revealed, when souls will rise up and call blessed such as led them to church and to Christ. "I was in your Sunday school class," or "I was saved by you as a brand plucked from the fire," or, "You gave me a word of encouragement when all others forsook me," such will be the expressions of heavenly gratitude the "bread cast upon the waters."

But what does all this teach us? It should teach us the better how to live. It should forcibly teach us that we must begin heaven here on earth if we would enjoy heaven above. Christ like earthly recognition means heavenly recognition, and the wise christian carefully practices this noble trait.

The more friends we have on earth in Christ, the more we are likely to have in heaven. Some need to learn "earthly recognition." There are needy people who are in want of a helping hand, a kind word, a smile of encouragement, who are yet being passed by daily without any recognition on the part of many christians. There are too many, who, like the Priest and Levite of old, pass heedlessly by such as need their tender sympathy and help.

We need more like the good old Samaritan who will get down from their high places into the dust and sand, and help the wounded at heart and soul. Many sad and cheerless hearts and homes might thus be transformed into "Edens" on earth. Seeing, therefore, just what God hath in store for those who love and faithfully serve Him, let us bring down a little more of heaven into daily life, beginning it thus while here on earth, for such will be surer of the same above, and will enjoy all the more the blessedness of heavenly recognition because they recognized people when on earth.

Dorcas has many to recognize in heaven, because she kindly recognized the poor and discouraged here in life. Josephine's body was followed by the ten thousand of France to its final resting place because she had been a friend to the ten thousand of France. And so heaven will be what we make it. Our present life will largely determine our future happiness in glory; some will enter heaven as "brands plucked from the fire," while others will "gain an abundant entrance."

When Mozart had written his last requiem, he turned to his daughter, and handing her the music said, "Daughter, play and sing this for me."

His daughter kindly took the music, and sitting down beside the piano, played and sang to the great satisfaction of him who requested the favor. After she had completed the song, she turned to see what effect it had upon her father. She saw a smile upon his face, but it was the fixed smile of death. While she played and sang, his soul took its winged flight to realms above.

Reader, be a friend to your fellowmen, be honest with yourself, and let your life be one so true to God, that when at last you fall asleep, it may be :

> "Asleep in Jesus ! blessed sleep,
> From which none ever wakes to weep ;
> A calm and undisturbed repose,
> Unbroken by the last of foes.
>
> Asleep in Jesus ! peaceful rest,
> Whose waking is supremely blest ;
> No fear, no woe, shall dim that hour
> That manifests the Saviour's power."

Thus, awaking from that last sleep, may your eyes behold the shining angels awaiting you, and may you hear your Blessed Master say unto you : "Well done, thou good and faithful servant; enter thou into the joys of thy Lord."

www.ingramcontent.com/pod-product-compliance
Lightning Source LLC
Chambersburg PA
CBHW032238080426
42735CB00008B/912